Alcohol Use Disorders

About the Authors

Stephen A. Maisto, PhD, ABPP (Clinical Psychology), is a Professor of Psychology at Syracuse University and is the Director of Research at the VA Center for Integrated Healthcare. He earned his PhD in experimental psychology in 1975 at the University of Wisconsin-Milwaukee and completed a postdoctoral respecialization in clinical psychology in 1985 at George Peabody College of Vanderbilt University. Dr. Maisto's research and clinical interests include the assessment and treatment of alcohol and other drug use disorders, HIV prevention, and the integration of behavioral health in the primary medical care setting. Dr. Maisto has authored or coauthored numerous journal articles, book chapters, and books.

Gerard J. Connors, PhD, ABPP, is Director of and a Senior Research Scientist at the Research Institute on Addictions at the University at Buffalo. He earned his doctoral degree in clinical psychology from Vanderbilt University in 1980. Dr. Connors' research interests include treatment of alcohol use disorders, relapse prevention, self-help group involvement, early interventions with heavy drinkers, and treatment evaluation. He is a fellow of the American Psychological Association (Divisions of Clinical Psychology and Addictions). Dr. Connors has authored or coauthored numerous scientific articles, books, and book chapters.

Ronda L. Dearing, PhD, is a Research Scientist at the Research Institute on Addictions at the University at Buffalo. She earned her PhD in clinical psychology from George Mason University in 2001. Dr. Dearing's research interests include help-seeking for alcohol and substance abuse, substance abuse treatment approaches, and the influences of shame and guilt on behavior and health. She is coauthor of the book *Shame and Guilt* (2002), and has authored or coauthored several scientific articles and chapters.

Advances in Psychotherapy – Evidence-Based Practice

Danny Wedding; PhD, MPH, Prof., St. Louis, MO
(Series Editor)
Larry Beutler; PhD, Prof., Palo Alto, CA
Kenneth E. Freedland; PhD, Prof., St. Louis, MO
Linda C. Sobell; PhD, ABPP, Prof., Ft. Lauderdale, FL
David A. Wolfe; PhD, Prof., Toronto
(Associate Editors)

The basic objective of this series is to provide therapists with practical, evidence-based treatment guidance for the most common disorders seen in clinical practice – and to do so in a "reader-friendly" manner. Each book in the series is both a compact "how-to-do" reference on a particular disorder for use by professional clinicians in their daily work, as well as an ideal educational resource for students and for practice-oriented continuing education.

The most important feature of the books is that they are practical and "reader-friendly:" All are structured similarly and all provide a compact and easy-to-follow guide to all aspects that are relevant in real-life practice. Tables, boxed clinical "pearls", marginal notes, and summary boxes assist orientation, while checklists provide tools for use in daily practice.

Alcohol Use Disorders

Stephen A. Maisto
Syracuse University and Center for Health and Behavior, Syracuse, NY

Gerard J. Connors
Research Institute on Addictions, University at Buffalo, Buffalo, NY

Ronda L. Dearing
Research Institute on Addictions, University at Buffalo, Buffalo, NY

HOGREFE

Library of Congress Cataloging in Publication

is available via the Library of Congress Marc Database under the
LC Control Number 2007932356

Library and Archives Canada Cataloguing in Publication

Maisto, Stephen A.
Alcohol use disorders / Stephen A. Maisto, Gerard J. Connors, Ronda L. Dearing.
(Advances in psychotherapy – evidence-based practice; v. 10)
Includes bibliographical references. ISBN 978-0-88937-317-4
1. Alcoholism—Treatment. I. Connors, Gerard Joseph II. Dearing, Ronda L III. Title. IV. Series.
RC565.M225 2007   616.86'106   C2007-904448-4

PUBLISHING OFFICES
USA: Hogrefe & Huber Publishers, 875 Massachusetts Avenue, 7th Floor,
                Cambridge, MA 02139
                Phone (866) 823-4726, Fax (617) 354-6875; E-mail info@hhpub.com
EUROPE: Hogrefe & Huber Publishers, Rohnsweg 25, 37085 Göttingen, Germany
                Phone +49 551 49609-0, Fax +49 551 49609-88, E-mail hh@hhpub.com

SALES & DISTRIBUTION
USA: Hogrefe & Huber Publishers, Customer Services Department,
                30 Amberwood Parkway, Ashland, OH 44805
                Phone (800) 228-3749, Fax (419) 281-6883, E-mail custserv@hhpub.com
EUROPE: Hogrefe & Huber Publishers, Rohnsweg 25, 37085 Göttingen, Germany
                Phone +49 551 49609-0, Fax +49 551 49609-88, E-mail hh@hhpub.com

OTHER OFFICES
CANADA: Hogrefe & Huber Publishers, 1543 Bayview Avenue, Toronto, Ontario M4G 3B5
SWITZERLAND: Hogrefe & Huber Publishers, Länggass-Strasse 76, CH-3000 Bern 9

Hogrefe & Huber Publishers
Incorporated and registered in the State of Washington, USA, and in Göttingen, Lower Saxony,
Germany

Printed and bound in the USA
ISBN 978-0-88937-317-4

Preface

Alcohol abuse and alcohol dependence are problems that have baffled clinicians, researchers, and policy makers for hundreds of years. Because of the effects of alcohol use disorders (AUDs) on individuals and the societies in which they live, advances in knowledge about them and in ways to ameliorate them have been high research priorities. In the last several decades this international research activity has paid off in the development of different methods of intervention for the AUDs that are effective and available to clinicians.

The purpose of this book is to further the effort to make empirically supported methods of AUD interventions more accessible to clinicians, whose daily patient/client care responsibilities may hinder their keeping up-to-date with the latest developments in clinical research and practice. The assessment and intervention procedures discussed in this book all have undergone extensive scrutiny and evaluation, both in a formal research sense and in actual clinical practice. They have been judged to be the best methods that the field has to offer clinicians in their attempts to improve the lives of those who come to them for help in reducing or stopping their consumption of alcohol. We hope that this book helps to make these methods the standard of clinical practice.

Acknowledgments

It is difficult to write an acknowledgments section of a book or even a journal article, because they are products of our professional growth over the years driven by what we have learned from many patients, students, teachers, and mentors. It will have to suffice here to express our unending gratitude to all of them. More immediately, we can name several individuals who have helped us and supported us in completing this book. We thank the Series Editor, Danny Wedding, PhD, and Robert Dimbleby of Hogrefe & Huber Publishers for their responsiveness to any and all of the questions we raised while completing this book. In addition, we thank Linda Sobell, PhD, ABPP, Series Associate Editor, for all of her guidance. Our appreciation also goes to Ms. Julie Pawlik, who made our manuscript presentable for public consumption, and to Mr. Mark Duerr for helping us write the test question items. Finally, SAM expresses his personal thanks to his wife Mary Jean, who forever seems to hear him talking about all of the projects sitting on his desk waiting to meet their deadlines. GJC expresses his personal thanks and appreciation to his wife, Lana Michaels Connors, and daughter Marissa for their unflagging love, support, and patience. RLD expresses her gratitude to GJC and SAM for including her on this project and for sharing their collective wisdom.

Dedication

To Safi
SAM

To Lana and Marissa
GJC

To my parents, Ron and Barbara Dearing
RLD

Table of Contents

1

Description of Alcohol Use Disorders

This book concerns empirically supported methods of assessment and psychotherapy of alcohol use disorders (alcohol abuse and alcohol dependence, in the terminology of the *Diagnostic and Statistical Manual of Mental Disorders*, Fourth Edition, Text Revision (DSM-IV-TR; American Psychiatric Association, 2000). Before proceeding with this chapter, it is important to specify some topics that the book will not cover that are related to its overall contents. First, in DSM-IV-TR terms, this book emphasizes assessment and treatment of the alcohol *use* disorders (AUDs), and not any of the other alcohol-*related* disorders that might be discussed, such as alcohol withdrawal, alcohol induced disorders, or alcohol intoxication. This is because the behavioral and psychological assessment and intervention methods described in this book were designed to address alcohol abuse and alcohol dependence, but not the other alcohol- related disorders that the latest DSM identifies.

Second, the assessment and treatment methods that this book includes have been evaluated with adults. Therefore, information on adolescents is excluded, because information about assessment and treatment obtained through evaluation of adult samples cannot be assumed to generalize to adolescents (usually defined as ages 12–18 years). Further, space limitations do not allow a full discussion of methods of assessment and psychotherapy with adolescents identified as having an AUD, as a considerable research and clinical literature has been generated on that topic, especially in the last 15 years.

Third, although this book primarily concerns behavioral and psychological interventions, we also discuss pharmacotherapies of AUDs. We have included medications treatment of the AUDs for two reasons. First, there is empirical support for the efficacy of selected pharmacotherapies of AUDs. Second, pharmacotherapies have been evaluated only in the context of their being used in combination with some kind of psychological or behavioral intervention or support, a few of which are among the empirically supported psychotherapies described in this book. Therefore, there is empirical support for the use of medications in combination with psychotherapies that have empirical support as stand-alone treatments. In this context, under specific conditions or in considering certain patient outcomes, a combined medication and psychotherapy intervention may show better patient outcomes than does the psychotherapy intervention alone.

With these preliminary comments done, we now proceed with description of the AUDs.

1.1   Terminology

The term "alcohol use disorders" denotes alcohol-related negative consequences, broadly defined

Alcohol use disorders is a generic term used to represent alcohol-related negative consequences or dysfunction, broadly defined. Over the past two centuries, efforts have been taken to define and classify such alcohol misuse, and particularly excessive consumption. Among the terms applied were delirium tremens, insanity caused by intemperance, inebriety, dipsomania (or drink seeking), and, in the mid-1800s, alcoholism (Grant & Dawson, 1999).

Most widely-used classification systems are the DSM and the ICD

The classification of misuse of alcohol today falls under the umbrella term of alcohol use disorders. The two most widely-used classification systems for alcohol-use disorders are the *Diagnostic and Statistical Manual of Mental Disorders*, Fourth Edition, Text Revision (DSM-IV-TR; American Psychiatric Association, 2000) and the tenth revision of the World Health Organization *International Classification of Diseases* (ICD-10; WHO, 1992). Both are categorical approaches to the assessment of AUDs, and both draw heavily from the concept of the alcohol dependence syndrome (Edwards & Gross, 1976).

1.2   Definition

Two categories of alcohol use disorders: alcohol dependence and alcohol abuse/ harmful use

There are two broad categories of alcohol use disorders within both the DSM and ICD classification systems. The first is *alcohol dependence*, and the second is *alcohol abuse* (in DSM) or *harmful use* (in ICD).

The DSM criteria for alcohol dependence are presented in Table 1. (They have been modified from their proposed use in the diagnosis of substance use disorders to reflect alcohol use and its consequences.) As evident in Table 1, a diagnosis of alcohol dependence is warranted when there is presentation of at least three indicants of impairment over the previous 12 months. Noteworthy is that indications of tolerance and/or withdrawal, two criteria closely associated with the concept of physical dependence on alcohol, do not need to be present in order to make a diagnosis of alcohol dependence. Thus, as noted in Table 1, there is the opportunity to subtype the diagnosis of alcohol dependence as being with physiological dependence (i.e., there is evidence of tolerance or withdrawal) or without physiological dependence (i.e., no evidence of tolerance or withdrawal).

The ICD criteria for alcohol dependence are outlined in Table 2. Similar to the DSM criteria, a diagnosis of alcohol dependence is warranted when a cluster of at least three relevant criteria have been documented at some time in the past 12 months.

The DSM and ICD nomenclatures offer provisions for an AUD that does not achieve the criteria associated with alcohol dependence. The criteria for such a disorder (called alcohol abuse in DSM and harmful use in ICD) are shown in Tables 3 and 4, respectively. As can be seen, the ICD harmful use category is focused on physical and psychological health damage. The DSM alcohol abuse category, in contrast, focuses as well on situations where social, legal, or vocational consequences have been documented. Nevertheless, their availability for use in assessment and diagnostic activities is valuable, as

Table 1
DSM-IV Criteria for Alcohol Dependence

A maladaptive pattern of alcohol use, leading to clinically significant impairment or distress, as manifested by three (or more) of the following, occurring at any time in the same 12-month period:

1. Tolerance, as defined by either of the following:
   (a) A need for markedly increased amounts of alcohol to achieve intoxication or desired effect.
   (b) Markedly diminished effect with continued use of the same amount of alcohol.
2. Withdrawal, as manifested by either of the following:
   (a) The characteristic withdrawal syndrome for alcohol.
   (b) Alcohol (or a closely related substance) is taken to relieve or avoid withdrawal symptoms.
3. Alcohol is often taken in larger amounts or over a longer period than was intended.
4. There is a persistent desire or unsuccessful efforts to cut down or control alcohol use.
5. A great deal of time is spent in activities necessary to obtain alcohol, use the substance, or recover from its effects.
6. Important social, occupational, or recreational activities are given up or reduced because of alcohol use.
7. The alcohol use is continued despite knowledge of having a persistent or recurrent physical or psychological problem that is likely to have been caused or exacerbated by alcohol (e.g., continued drinking despite recognition that an ulcer was made worse by alcohol consumption).

Adapted from American Psychiatric Association (2000)

Table 2
ICD-10 Criteria for Alcohol Dependence

A diagnosis of alcohol dependence should usually be made only if three or more of the following have been experienced or exhibited at some time during the previous year:

1. A strong desire or sense of compulsion to consume alcohol.
2. Difficulties in controlling alcohol consumption in terms of its onset, termination, or levels of use.
3. A physiological withdrawal state when alcohol use has ceased or been reduced, as evidenced by: the characteristic withdrawal syndrome for alcohol; or use of alcohol (or a closely related substance) with the intention of relieving or avoiding withdrawal symptoms.
4. Evidence of tolerance, such that increased doses of alcohol are required in order to achieve effects originally produced by lower doses.
5. Progressive neglect of alternative pleasures or interests because of alcohol use, increased amount of time necessary to obtain or drink alcohol or to recover from its effects.
6. Persisting with alcohol use despite clear evidence of overtly harmful consequences, such as harm to the liver through excessive drinking, depressive mood states consequent to periods of heavy drinking, or alcohol-related impairment of cognitive functioning; efforts should be made to determine that the user was actually, or could be expected to be, aware of the nature and extent of the harm.

Adapted from World Health Organization (1992)

Table 3
DSM-IV Criteria for Alcohol Abuse

A. A maladaptive pattern of alcohol use leading to clinically significant impairment or distress, as manifested by one (or more) of the following, occurring within a 12-month period:
   1. Recurrent alcohol use resulting in a failure to fulfill major role obligations at work, school, or home (e.g., repeated absences or poor work performance related to alcohol use; alcohol-related absences, suspensions, or expulsions from school; neglect of children or household).
   2. Recurrent alcohol use in situations in which it is physically hazardous (e.g., driving an automobile or operating a machine when impaired by alcohol use).
   3. Recurrent alcohol-related legal problems (e.g., arrests for alcohol-related disorderly conduct).
   4. Continued alcohol use despite having persistent or recurrent social or interpersonal problems caused or exacerbated by the effects of alcohol (e.g., arguments with spouse about consequences of intoxication, physical fights).

B. The symptoms have never met the criteria for alcohol dependence.

Adapted from American Psychiatric Association (2000)

Table 4
ICD-10 Criteria for Harmful Use

The ICD diagnosis of harmful use requires a pattern of alcohol use that is causing damage to health. The diagnosis requires evidence of actual damage to the mental or physical health of the user. The harmful use diagnosis should not be used if alcohol dependence is present.

Adapted from World Health Organization (1992)

they permit identification of at-risk or harmful uses of alcohol, regardless of whether the criteria for alcohol dependence have been achieved.

1.2.1   Implications for Clinical Practice

Implications of the alcohol abuse/ harmful use diagnosis for clinical practice

The concepts of alcohol abuse (in DSM) and harmful use (in ICD) have significant implications for clinical practice. Implicit in these concepts is the appreciation that *alcohol consumption falls on a continuum*, ranging from limited consumption to very heavy consumption. Further, a variety of alcohol-related consequences are possible at any level of alcohol consumption. In this regard, alcohol consequences, like alcohol consumption, fall on a continuum, ranging from no consequences to very serious consequences, whether they be physical, social, family, legal, or occupational. While there is a general linear relationship between consumption and problems (with greater consumption being associated with more negative consequences), it cannot be assumed that lower levels of alcohol use will result in only trivial problems. There are many cases where infrequent and generally not heavy drinkers will experience severe negative consequences associated with their drinking, and many cases where heavier drinkers might experience relatively fewer negative consequences. As such, alcohol consumption and associated consequences both need to be assessed.

1.3   Epidemiology

Approximately 2 billion people worldwide consume alcoholic beverages, among whom 76.3 million (3.8%) are estimated to have a diagnosable alcohol use disorder (WHO, 2004). The personal and societal costs associated with problematic drinking are considerable, in terms of both morbidity and mortality, in almost all parts of the world. According to the World Health Organization (2004), alcohol use is linked annually to 1.8 million deaths (3.2% of total deaths worldwide) and a loss of over 58 million (4% of the total) disability-adjusted "life years."

Alcohol consumption, alcohol use disorders, and negative consequences are not distributed uniformly from country to country. Per capita consumption, for example, is highest in Europe (between 10 and 11 liters of pure alcohol annually), followed by the Americas (between 6 and 7 liters) (WHO, 2004). The lowest per capita rates of consumption were reported for Southeast Asia and in regions heavily populated by Muslims. Estimates calculated by the World Health Organization (2004) also reveal variations in the prevalence of alcohol dependence among adults in different countries. Highest rates of alcohol dependence were estimated for Poland, Brazil, and Peru (all between 10–12% of adults).

The prevalence of alcohol abuse and alcohol dependence has been studied in depth in the United States. Based on national survey data gathered in 2001–2002, the 12-month prevalence rates for alcohol abuse and alcohol dependence were 4.65% and 3.81%, respectively (Grant, Dawson, Stinson, Chou, Dufour, & Pickering, 2004). Supplemental analyses reported by Grant et al. provided several indications about prevalence rates by sex, race-ethnicity, and age. With regard to alcohol abuse, the 12-month prevalence was greater among men (6.93%) than women (2.55%). This pronounced gender difference was statistically significant among Whites, Blacks, and Hispanics. While the same pattern was evident among Native Americans and Asians, it was not statistically significant. The gender difference was statistically significant within all age groups among Whites, Blacks, and Hispanics (except among Hispanics aged 65 and older, where the pattern was evident but not statistically significant). In terms of race-ethnicity, alcohol abuse was more prevalent among Whites (5.10%) relative to Blacks (3.29%), Asians (2.13%), and Hispanics (3.97%). Further, the rate of alcohol abuse was significantly greater among Native Americans (5.75%) and Hispanics (3.97%) when compared to Asians (2.13%). Finally, in terms of age, the prevalence of alcohol abuse decreased with the advancement of age.

In terms of alcohol dependence, the 12-month prevalence overall was significantly greater among men (5.42%) than among women (2.32%). While this pattern was evident for all race-ethnicity groups, the gender difference was statistically significant among Whites, Blacks, and Hispanics only. Further, Whites (3.83%), Native Americans (6.35%), and Hispanics (3.95%) had higher rates of alcohol dependence relative to Asians (2.41%). Finally, in terms of age, rates of alcohol dependence decreased as age increased. This pattern was evident for the population as a whole and also among men and women separately.

3.8% of people worldwide have an alcohol use disorder

1.4 Course and Prognosis

The course and prognosis for persons with an alcohol use disorder will vary from person to person, with considerable variability present among treatment seekers and nontreatment seekers. Several studies described below provide insights on the outcomes for each of these populations.

Based on general population surveys, the incidence of initial alcohol use begins to rise steeply at around 14 years of age. Alcohol misuse initially occurs most often in adolescence through the early 30s, and individuals who experience few adverse consequences of drinking by age 35 generally are unlikely to develop alcohol dependence (Grant, 1997). The initial presentation for treatment of alcohol dependence by both men and women is often in the early 40s, following many years of alcohol-related dysfunction (Schuckit, Anthenelli, Bucholz, Hesselbrock, & Tipp, 1995; Schuckit, Daeppen, Tipp, Hesselbrock, & Bucholz, 1998).

Alcohol dependence typically is characterized by remissions and relapses, and not by continuous daily drinking. A significant proportion of alcohol dependent individuals, estimated at minimum to be 25%, will experience long-term or permanent remission without utilization of treatment (Dawson, Grant, Stinson, Chou, Huang, & Juan, 2005; Sobell, Cunningham, & Sobell, 1996). Others will seek treatment in specialty settings or attend self-help groups, with a 40% to 60% probability of long-term remission (American Psychiatric Association, 1994; Schuckit, Smith, Danko, Bucholz, Reich, & Bierut, 2001). A substantial proportion of individuals will experience persistent dependence with or without treatment.

A pair of recent reports provide some insights into the clinical course of alcohol use disorders. In the first report, Schuckit et al. (2001) conducted assessments on 1,346 predominantly blue-collar men and women, and then reassessed them 5 years later. Of the 298 identified as alcohol dependent at baseline, 36.9% continued to be so diagnosed at the 5-year follow-up (based on continuing to meet at least three of the seven DSM-IV criteria for alcohol dependence). Approximately two-thirds of the 298 continued to experience at least one or more of the 11 DSM-IV abuse or dependence criteria over the 5-year follow-up period. Of the 288 individuals who at baseline met the criteria for alcohol abuse, 36.1% continued to achieve the criteria five years later; 54.9% reported at least one of the 11 alcohol abuse/dependence criteria during the follow-up period. Only 3.5% of the alcohol abuse population at baseline met the alcohol dependence criteria 5 years later, suggesting that alcohol abusers do not exhibit an inevitable progression from abuse to full-blown alcohol dependence. Finally, among the 760 individuals who at baseline had no alcohol diagnosis, only 2.5% subsequently met the criteria for alcohol dependence, and 12.8% met the criteria for alcohol abuse. Taken together, these findings suggest a stability of alcohol-related dysfunction over time among individuals with a diagnosis of alcohol dependence. A diagnosis of alcohol abuse predicted a milder, less persistent disorder over time, with infrequent progression to alcohol dependence.

A more recent study provides additional insights. Dawson et al. (2005) used data from a large epidemiological study focusing on recovery from DSM-IV-defined alcohol dependence. Specifically, they examined the past year status of 4,422 individuals who had met the criteria for alcohol dependence prior to the past year (PPY). Among those classified as PPY alcohol dependent, 25% remained classified as dependent in the past year, 27.3% were in partial remission, 11.8% were asymptomatic risk drinkers whose drinking pattern indicated a risk of relapse, 17.7% were low-risk drinkers, and 18.2% were abstainers.

One quarter of the PPY alcohol dependent participants in the Dawson et al. (2005) study reported ever having sought help (e.g., outpatient treatment, Alcoholics Anonymous) for their drinking. Among the 1,205 who ever received treatment, 35.1% were abstinent in the past year, compared to 12.4% in the never treated group. If one were to consider the asymptomatic risk drinkers, the low-risk drinkers, and those abstinent as in "full remission" in the past year, the rate of full remission was higher in the ever treated group (51.2%) than in the never treated group (46.5%). Although conclusions about the direct effects of treatment on these past year outcomes cannot confidently be drawn from these data, they do indicate a substantial degree of recovery from alcohol dependence.

The prognosis for treatment of an alcohol use disorder has been addressed in the context of both shorter-term (12 months) and longer-term (up to decades) treatment. The shorter-term category was assessed by Miller, Walters, and Bennett (2001), who studied the outcomes for over 8,000 patients who participated in seven large multisite AUD treatment projects. They found that during the year after treatment, around 25% of the patients were continuously abstinent and another 10% used alcohol moderately without problems. As such, one third had fully positive outcomes. Even among those who consumed alcohol during the follow-up year (this includes the previously-mentioned 10% who used alcohol moderately without problems), substantial improvements were noted. In this regard, patients who drank at all during the follow-up year nevertheless were abstinent, on average, three out of every four days, representing an average increase in abstinent days, from before to after treatment, of 128%. As a group, their overall alcohol consumption dropped 87% from before to after treatment. Finally, alcohol-related problems across all participants studied decreased by 60%. Taken together, these data provide a foundation for optimism regarding 12-month outcomes following treatment for alcohol problems.

Research provides a strong foundation for optimism in the treatment of alcohol use disorders, based on 12-month outcomes following alcoholism treatment

The issue of long-term outcomes was reviewed by Finney, Moos, & Timko (1999). They summarized the findings of 12 studies published in the 1980s and 1990s that provided data on remission rates. Remission was defined as abstinence, nonproblem drinking, or "substantially improved drinking," and the follow-up periods ranged from 8 to 20 years. Across these studies, remission rates ranged from 21% to 83%. These rates need to be considered with caution because it is not possible to draw a causal inference relating treatment to the long-term remission rates reported.

1.5 Differential Diagnosis

The AUDs may be confused with either "normal" or "nonpathological" drinking, such as in "social drinking." Nonpathological use of alcohol does not feature symptoms like high tolerance to alcohol, alcohol withdrawal symp-

Differentiating AUDs from "normal" or "nonpathological" drinking

toms with a drop in the blood alcohol level, compulsive alcohol use, or recurrent negative consequences of alcohol use that characterize alcohol abuse or alcohol dependence. As noted in DSM-IV-TR, frequent alcohol intoxication invariably is part of alcohol abuse or alcohol dependence, but incidents of intoxication alone do not meet criteria for an AUD diagnosis.

However, individuals who drink beyond certain quantities of alcohol at a particular frequency may be identified as "at risk" (for incurring alcohol problems, or an AUD). These individuals, also identified as "hazardous drinkers," have become highly visible to the field as clinicians have become aware of their larger numbers in the population than the prevalence of individuals with an AUD. Furthermore, as we will show later in this book, in the last 20 years a segment of clinical research and practice has been devoted to methods of identifying hazardous drinkers and of intervening to modify their patterns of alcohol use toward primary prevention of the development of alcohol abuse or dependence.

1.6   Comorbidities

Several psychiatric disorders have a high rate of co-occurrence with AUDs

Besides the medical complications that may be associated with chronic, heavy alcohol consumption, the following psychiatric disorders have a disproportionately high rate of cooccurrence with the AUDs (APA, 2000): mood disorders, anxiety disorders, schizophrenia, and antisocial personality disorder.

1.7   Diagnostic Procedures and Documentation

Research has been extremely productive in helping to develop psychometrically-sound methods designed to provide DSM- (and ICD) based AUD (and other substance use and psychiatric) diagnoses, as well as measures that reflect the criteria that constitute an AUD diagnosis. As we described earlier, the content of the criteria for alcohol abuse and alcohol dependence in the DSM was heavily influenced by the alcohol dependence syndrome construct, and this is apparent in the content of the measures that we include here.

Several psychometrically sound methods are available for determining the presence of an AUD diagnosis

Table 5 lists psychometrically sound methods of determining an AUD diagnosis that reflect several of the criteria that constitute a diagnosis of alcohol abuse or dependence. We also include methods of measuring alcohol consumption, which are important for monitoring patients' clinical course but that are not directly relevant to making an AUD diagnosis according to DSM criteria. The information in Table 5 is adapted from chapters by Maisto, McKay, and Tiffany (2003) and by Sobell and Sobell (2003), and it can be extremely valuable to clinicians in their efforts to derive case formulations of their patients' alcohol problem severity and to monitor its course over time. Source references and full descriptive information for all of the measures listed in Table 5 are included in the Maisto et al. and Sobell and Sobell chapters, and in the book where the chapters are published (Allen & Wilson, 2003). It also is important to note that the measures listed in Table 5 are not the only ones available to measure the variables represented in Table 5. However, they were included because of their good psychometric properties and their widespread use in the field.

Table 5
Measures to Diagnose AUDs and that Reflect AUD Diagnostic Criteria

Measure	Purpose
Diagnostic Interview Schedule for DSM-IV	To provide a structured measure of DSM-IV AUD Criteria
Substance Abuse Module, Version 4.1	More detailed substance abuse section of the Composite International Diagnostic Interview, a semi-structured interview for assessment of DSM-IV and ICD-10 diagnostic criteria
Alcohol Dependence Scale	To measure the severity of alcohol dependence based on the alcohol dependence syndrome construct
Ethanol Dependence Scale	To measure elements of the alcohol dependence syndrome
Substance Dependence Severity Scale	To provide a measure of dependence that is free of cultural bias
Drinker Inventory of Consequences	To provide a measure of consequences of alcohol use
Drinking Problems Index	To provide a measure of alcohol-related problems in adults aged 55 years and older
Impaired Control Scale	To provide a measure of actual and perceived control over alcohol consumption
Temptation and Restraint Inventory	To provide a measure of preoccupation with control over drinking
Alcohol Craving Questionnaire	To provide a measure of acute alcohol craving
Quantity-Frequency Scales	To provide quickly-obtained information on number of days drinking and amount of alcohol consumption
Timeline Follow-Back Interview, Form 90	To provide measures of daily drinking

2

Theories and Models of Alcohol Use Disorders

The definitions and descriptions of alcohol use disorders (AUDs) presented in Chapter 1 give the basis for our describing current ways that clinicians and researchers *understand* AUDs. By "understand," we mean perception of factors that affect the development of a disorder, its maintenance, and its modification. Such information is critical for this book, because how clinicians think about and understand a problem may directly affect how they assess its manifestations and intervene to change it.

2.1   Traditional Theories of AUDs

A number of theories have been proposed to explain AUDs

Until recently, researchers and clinicians alike usually sought a single-factor explanation of what causes and maintains alcohol problems. Miller and Hester (2003) provided an excellent review of these models/theories. They summarized 12 single-factor models by describing each one, identifying its major emphasis about the cause and maintenance of AUDs, and citing an example of an intervention to modify AUD-related behavior that follows from the model. These 12 models span the biological, psychological, and social/environmental domains, and the etiological factors include individual characteristics (e.g., genetics, personality characteristics, lack of knowledge, motivation), environmental effects (e.g., cultural norms), and the interaction between the individual and their environment (e.g., family dynamics, social learning). Due to the wide variety of causal factors, AUD assessment and intervention differ considerably for each model. Treatment approaches vary widely also, and include interventions such as moral suasion, spiritual growth, restriction of alcohol supply, confrontation, coping skills training, and family therapy. It is here that we see why awareness of how the clinician understands AUDs is so important: If it guides what clinicians do with their patients, then the content, process, and outcomes could differ in major ways.

Through about the first three-quarters of the twentieth century, AUD theories frequently outpaced the data necessary to evaluate them. More recently, the quality of research in each of these domains has improved considerably, and each of these "single-factor" theories has been found to have some merit. Nevertheless, each set of factors alone, biological, psychological, or social/environmental, has been found lacking in its attempt to provide a satisfactory explanation of the AUDs.

2.2   Biopsychosocial Model of AUDs

Empirical evidence and a newer way of conceptualizing health and illness merged in the latter twentieth century to lead to the generation and broad influence of a *"biopsychosocial" model of AUDs*. Besides dissatisfaction with the account of AUDs that single factor theories provided, there were several other manifestations of alcohol problems that have been influential. In this regard, in the important report by the Institute of Medicine (IOM, 1990), three main features of alcohol problems were highlighted that led the authors of that report to the conclusion that there is no one "alcoholism" that is a unitary "disease." Instead, alcohol problems are heterogeneous in their manifestation and etiology. Specifically, the IOM report argues that research conducted primarily since the early 1970s had shown that alcohol problems are, first, heterogeneous in their presentation, that is, they might be thought of as a syndrome with a variety of symptoms (Shaffer, LaPlante, LaBrie, Kidman, Donato, & Stanton, 2004; Vaillant, 1983). Second, alcohol problems are heterogeneous in their course. This conclusion is in contrast to more traditional ideas of alcoholism as a unitary, progressive disease. In fact, the course of alcohol problems can vary significantly, as shown by many longitudinal studies, and may or may not be characterized by "progressivity." Third, alcohol problems are heterogeneous in etiology. This conclusion rests on the findings that no single cause or set of causes of alcohol problems has been identified. Rather, individuals who are identified as having alcohol problems present with diverse developmental trajectories of AUDs that are likely the result of the confluence of biological, psychological, and social factors. No single factor, set of factors, or factor domain has etiological priority of importance over another, none is necessary or sufficient in any case, and the influence of any factor or set of factors in AUD development varies across individuals.

The strength of the research and clinical evidence behind these conclusions along with newer conceptions of illness and health that rose to prominence in the 1970s have led to the current wide-spread influence of the "biopsychosocial" (BPS) model of AUDs. Engel (1977, 1980) presented the BPS model first to psychiatry and the rest of medicine and argued its superiority to the prevailing "biomedical" model in the treatment of patients presenting with medical or psychiatric disorders. Similar to conclusions that the IOM (1990) articulated about alcohol problems, Engel (1977) argued that to view a patient presenting to physicians with some medical or psychiatric disorder in one dimension (whether it be purely biological, psychological, or social) results in the likely result of missing significant aspects of the patient's problem and thus its amelioration. Engel argued that health, and thus illness, is best viewed as the outcome of nonrecursive (bidirectional causality, such that change in "A" causes change in "B," which in turn causes change in "A") interactions among the hierarchical components of biological, individual, family, and community systems, and of components within those systems. Moreover, "lower order" components (biological) are subsumed by "higher order" (e.g., community) systems. Engel argued that this level of complexity is essential to understanding illness and its manifestations. Figure 1, from Engel (1980), illustrates this thinking.

The biopsychosocial model is the approach most widely endorsed today

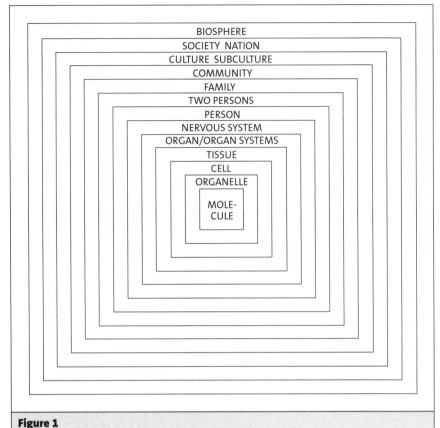

Figure 1
Continuum of Natural Systems (Engel, 1980)
Reprinted with permission from the American Journal of Psychiatry (© 1980), American Psychiatric Association.

In 1988, Donovan discussed the "emerging" acceptance of a BPS model among alcohol clinical practitioners and researchers. In 2005, Donovan expressed the tenor of the field by noting that the BPS model of alcohol problems is no longer emerging but has emerged. This raises the question of what variables must actually be considered in understanding any instance of presentation of AUDs. O'Brien (2001) provided a summary in response to this question in his listing of important BPS factors in the "onset" and continuation of not only AUDs, but of other substance use disorders as well. O'Brien's list of variables is divided into three classes: agent (drugs), host (user), and environment.

The variables included in the *agent* category include *substance availability* (especially important in illicit substances), *cost of the substance*, *substance purity or potency*, and *mode of substance administration*, such as oral, nasal, or intravenous. The *host* variables include factors such as *innate tolerance to a substance*, i.e., the tolerance that an individual shows to a substance the first time that he or she uses it. Other tolerance-related factors include *speed of acquiring tolerance to a substance* and the *likelihood of experiencing pleasure when using a substance*. Another host factor is the speed and efficiency with which an individual *metabolizes a substance*. An individual's *psychiatric symptoms* also may affect the onset and continuation of substance use, as might *prior experiences with a substance and expectations* about the consequences of using it. Finally, the tendency for an individual to engage in *risky behaviors* also may affect substance use.

Environmental factors may range from the immediate setting of substance use to macro-environmental factors. Therefore, for example, the social setting may affect substance use, as might community attitudes. Included in the latter are peer influences and role models. Another environmental factor that O'Brien (2001) identified is availability of sources of pleasure or recreation (more generally, sources of positive reinforcement) besides substance use. Opportunities for employment or education also might be associated with substance use. Finally, after repeated use of a substance, cues in the environment may become strongly conditioned to substance use so that they become stimuli that elicit or trigger the desire to use that substance(s). It is notable in scanning O'Brien's list of variables that each of them has empirical support for its importance. Nevertheless, none of these variables alone can explain the development and maintenance of the AUDs.

In summary, the empirical evidence points clearly to the AUDs as complex and multiply determined, so that the BPS model seems to have the best chance to productively guide clinical practice and research on the AUDs. However, if we take the next steps in better specifying what this conclusion may mean for the everyday clinical practice of clinicians, the directions that the BPS model takes us may not be apparent. In this regard, the BPS model may seem so broad that deriving specific ideas for assessment and intervention is a major undertaking with a low likelihood of success. We have summarized the influential clinical implications of the BPS model in Table 6.

We will see the influence of the BPS model in the remainder of this book in our discussions of methods of assessment and intervention for the AUDs. In particular, our approach to assessment and treatment planning takes a multivariate perspective, and we describe and discuss a "menu" of empirically supported AUD treatment methods. The development of each treatment method

Table 6
Implications of the BPS Model for Clinical Practice

1. *Individualized assessment and treatment planning.* If no two cases of AUDs can be presumed to be alike in manifestation, etiology, or course, then adequate clinical care depends on individualized evaluation and assessment.

2. *No one "prescribed" treatment.* It may be that more than one intervention or treatment technique may have empirical support or be preferred for use with a given patient. There is no one "mandated" intervention that works for everyone.

3. *Menu of interventions.* It follows from (2) above, and as Miller and Hester (2003) noted, having a "menu" of intervention options available makes the most clinical sense. In addition, combining "levels" of intervention, as Engel (1980) called them, say pharmacotherapy and family therapy, may be necessary in intervening with a given individual. This menu-based approach is consistent with a "stepped care" model of treatment (as suggested by Sobell & Sobell, 2000), which involves tailoring the intensity of treatment to an individual's level of severity and subsequent treatment response, in order to provide the least invasive and least expensive form of intervention.

that we describe in Chapter 4 was guided primarily by one of the models or theories discussed at the beginning of this chapter, and we will discuss those origins. Accordingly, despite evidence for meeting criteria for "empirically supported," none of the methods that we discuss in Chapter 4 alone is necessary or sufficient as a generally effective AUD treatment, but each may constitute a component of an effective intervention plan for any given individual being treated in a given context.

3

Diagnosis and Treatment Indications

3.1   Introduction

In the previous two chapters, we provided information on diagnostic criteria for alcohol use disorders, differential diagnosis, and models and theories that serve as frameworks for conceptualizing alcohol-related problems. In this chapter, we provide guidance on the assessment/evaluation process, the development of the treatment plan, and treatment indications.

3.2   General Guidelines and Considerations

The collection of assessment information and the development of a treatment plan are best viewed as a collaborative undertaking. As such, those processes should be highly interactive. In addition, the therapist should be active in instilling optimism, facilitating motivation, and helping the patient mobilize his or her resources in service of the change process.

Assessment and the development of the treatment plan should be a collaborative undertaking

3.3   Drinking History

It is critical to obtain a *comprehensive and detailed drinking history*, covering the patient's lifetime drinking history as well as current drinking and associated problems. In the following sections, we identify and briefly describe the major assessment domains relevant to the collection of a complete drinking history.

3.3.1   Alcohol Consumption

The assessment of alcohol consumption predominantly revolves around the determination of the *frequency of drinking* and the *amount of alcohol being consumed* during these drinking occasions. Some clinicians find it helpful to use a calendar procedure, called the Timeline Follow-Back (TLFB), popularized by Sobell and Sobell (1992). Essentially, the therapist and patient collaborate on inserting into calendar boxes the amount of alcohol consumed (in *standard drinks*) on a day-by-day basis for a particular pretreatment period, such as the past month or the 30 days preceding the patient's last drinking day.

> **Clinical Pearl**
> **Standard Drink Chart**
>
> A standard drink consists of 0.6 ounces of ethanol, as contained in:
>   12 ounces of 5% alcohol beer
>   5 ounces of 12% alcohol table wine
>   1.5 ounces of 40% hard liquor
>
> (A paper by Miller, Heather, and Hall, 1991, provides a convenient listing of conversions of typically-cited quantities of alcohol in beverages for American and metric systems.)

The drinking history assessment includes evaluation of alcohol consumption and alcohol related consequences

Because it is important for the therapist and patient to be using the same metric for a drink, standard drink charts are generally used (see above). If a patient reports consumption of a mixed drink containing 2 ounces of alcohol, two standard drinks would be reported. Patients are instructed to record "special days" on the calendar, such as birthdays, vacations, parties, etc., to help trigger their memory regarding alcohol consumption. Free downloadable instructions and calendars for administration of the TLFB are available from the Guided Self-Change Web site (www.nova.edu/gsc).

A variety of useful information can be derived from the completed calendar, such as the percentage of days drinking versus abstinent, the percentage of days drinking heavily (often defined as a day during which five standard

November 2006		1 2	2 (10)	3 (15)	4 (16)
					Bowling
5 (5)	6 0	7 0	8 (9)	9 2	10 (12)	11 (12)
			Birthday			
12 (5)	13 0	14 0	15 3	16 (6)	17 (15)	18 (12)
19 3	20 0	21 0	22 (5)	23 (9)	24 (10)	25 (14)
				Thanksgiving		
26 (5)	27 0	28 2	29 3	30 2		

Figure 2
Example Timeline Calendar (with Heavy Drinking Days Circled)

drinks are consumed by a man or four by a woman), and the patterning of drinking (e.g., does drinking occur on only certain days of the week?). A sample calendar month is provided in Figure 2. Other information also can be gathered and recorded on the calendar. For example, it is sometimes useful to record if the patient was drinking alone or with others and where the drinking occurred. This might reveal useful treatment-planning associations, such as heavy drinking typically occurring at specific locations or when drinking with particular individuals. Finally, it may be useful to identify what period of time the drinking occurred so as to be in a position to calculate roughly the blood alcohol levels being reached when drinking.

In addition to the collection of current drinking information, it will be useful to gather other drinking history data. Examples include asking about how many years the patient has been concerned about his or her drinking, how many years it has been a problem, age began drinking, age of first intoxication, and the extent to which the current drinking pattern is similar or dissimilar to the patient's previous drinking patterns.

3.3.2   Alcohol-Related Consequences

Consequences associated with drinking, recent as well as lifetime, can be assessed in *multiple domains of functioning*. A useful history of domains of drinking consequences has been provided by Miller, Tonigan, and Longabaugh (1995), who developed the Drinker Inventory of Consequences (DrInC). The domains of consequences, and samples of consequences from each of these domains, are described in the box below. An assessment of such consequences should be made for a lifetime frame and for a more recent period, such as the last six months. A shorter, 15-item version of the DrInC, the Short Inventory of Problems (SIP, Miller et al., 1995) is provided in the Appendix.

There are several other physical consequences that should be assessed, including tolerance and any history of withdrawal symptoms following past cessation of drinking. In addition, it often is useful to ask patients about their degree of craving for alcohol, and how frequently and where such craving is most evident. One useful standardized instrument for assessing craving is the Alcohol Craving Questionnaire – Short Form – Revised (ACQ–SF–R; Singleton, 1997). The ACQ–SF–R is in the public domain and is available from the author or in the downloadable NIAAA publication, *Assessing Alcohol Problems: A Guide for Clinicians and Researchers* (Allen & Wilson, 2003). Finally, to assess for other possible sequelae of alcohol consumption, arrangements for a laboratory work-up and/or physical exam should be made.

Clinical Pearl
Domains of Drinking Consequences

Physical
- Hangover or felt bad after drinking.
- Trouble sleeping after drinking.
- Sick and vomiting after drinking.
- Sex life has suffered because of drinking.

Clinical Pearl (continued)

Interpersonal
- Family or friends have worried or complained about the drinking.
- Ability to be a good parent has suffered.
- Said or did embarrassing things while drinking.
- Marriage or love relationship has been harmed.
- Social life has been damaged.

Intrapersonal
- Have felt bad about myself because of drinking.
- Have guilt or felt ashamed because of drinking.
- Have not had the life I want because of my drinking.
- Drinking has gotten in the way of my growth.

Impulse Control
- Have driven after drinking.
- Have taken foolish risks after drinking.
- Trouble with the law because of my drinking.
- Have broken things while intoxicated.
- Have had an accident because of my drinking.

Social Responsibility
- Have missed work or school because of my drinking.
- Quality of my work has suffered because of my drinking.
- Have had money problems because of my drinking.
- Fired from or left a job or school because of my drinking.

Adapted from Miller et al. (1995)

3.3.3   Other Drug Use

The nature and extent of other drug use needs to be assessed

The nature and extent of other drug use should be assessed. Classes of substances that can be included in this assessment include marijuana, tranquilizers, sedatives, stimulants, cocaine, crack cocaine, hallucinogens, and opiates. The use of these drugs can be recorded on the calendar described earlier. Information on the use of tobacco products also should be gathered.

3.3.4   Pros and Cons of Drinking

It is useful to have patients describe the advantages as well as disadvantages of drinking, and, in turn, the advantages and disadvantages of quitting drinking. In both cases, it is possible to develop a sense as to conflicting "pushes" to drink or quit. Often described as a *decisional balance*, it is anticipated that the scale will tip in the direction of quitting when the advantages of not drinking outweigh the advantages of continuing to drink. A sample decisional balance exercise for use with patients is provided in the Appendix. Identification of additional advantages versus disadvantages of drinking also can be elicited by asking patients to describe their reasons for stopping drinking.

Clinical Pearl
Instructions for Using the Decisional Balance Exercise (Sample Wording)

Therapist: I'd like to have you make a list of the pros and cons of drinking and the pros and cons of stopping drinking. Another way to think about this is in terms of costs and benefits – think about the costs and benefits of drinking and the costs and benefits of stopping drinking. After you have written down all of the costs and benefits, we'll use these lists to help you weigh the pros and cons of continuing to drink as compared to stopping drinking. These lists will help you decide whether it makes sense to stop drinking. Often we just continue in our regular routines, without really thinking about costs and benefits. But, when we're thinking of making any type of change, we often use this same process to weigh the pros and cons of the decision. Maybe we don't write out the lists, but we use this type of thinking to make the decision. Let me give you an example. If you were thinking of accepting a new job, you would probably think through the pros and cons of your current job and compare them to the pros and cons of the new job. Then, you would make the decision based on whether the benefits of changing are greater (as compared to the costs) than the benefits of staying at the same job. Does this make sense? (Wait for response and offer clarification as necessary.) A couple of things to think about while making your lists are: What are some of the possible consequences of continuing your current drinking patterns? What are some of the things that you enjoy about drinking? What might be different if you were to stop drinking?

(Give the patient time to develop their lists. This may require some prompting. If a patient is struggling with any of the categories, it might be helpful to provide them with some examples that they have already shared during the clinical dialogue. Once the patient has completed the four lists, use the information he or she has provided to help them compare the pros and cons of drinking versus quitting, as described in the dialogue below.)

Therapist: Okay, so now that you have your lists, I'd like you to take a minute to compare the benefits to the costs. One thing that is important to remember is that the decision of whether to change is up to you. Based on your lists, can you tell me whether it seems like the costs of continuing your current patterns are worth it? If these were the pros and cons of changing jobs, would it be a hard decision to make?

(Continue to explore the decisional balance, accepting the fact that there may be some ambivalence, as there often is with any decision.)

Note: The above wording can be modified slightly to reflect a drinking moderation goal, rather than an abstinence goal.

Clinical Pearl
Clinical Advantages of Completing a Decisional Balance

- Addresses patients' ambivalence in a structured manner by having them evaluate the pros and cons of changing their drinking.
- Examines all aspects of a behavior – good things and less good things.
- Helps establish the goal of tipping the scale in favor of change.
- Increases the salience of the negatives and positives of change.
- Makes patients more aware of the costs and benefits.
- Creates a positive atmosphere to discuss change.
- Provides a framework for assessment, goal setting, and discussion of behavior change.

3.3.5   Motivational Readiness to Change

Motivation falls on a continuum, and vacillates over time

Motivational readiness to change is thought to be central to the behavior change process. Indeed, it is hard to imagine meaningful behavioral change in the absence of motivation to change. However, *motivation falls on a continuum and usually vacillates over time*. Because of its potential value in the assessment process, efforts have been taken to design "readiness ladders" to assess motivation to change. An example of a readiness ruler is shown in Figure 3. A copy of this ruler is provided in the Appendix for use with patients. Once the patient has identified his or her level of readiness using the ruler, the clinician can use the patient's readiness rating as a starting point for discussions about change. For example, at lower levels of readiness, clinicians might express concern and offer information about hazardous drinking. If the patient's readiness ruler indicates that he or she is unsure about changing, the clinician can attempt to elicit the pros and cons of drinking (as in the Decisional Balance exercise described previously) or can ask the patient what it would take to move to a higher number. If the patient conveys a high level of readiness, the clinician can help the patient develop a plan for change including identification of any needed resources (Center for Substance Abuse Treatment, 1999). Such assessments can be administered at whatever frequency appears warranted, including doing so at each treatment session.

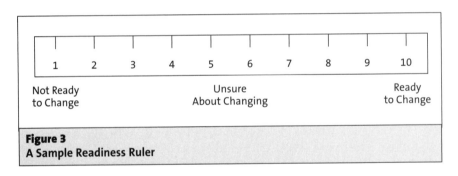

Figure 3
A Sample Readiness Ruler

Less than optimal motivation is often amenable to change, and a number of motivational interventions have been proposed to increase the likelihood of patients actively maintaining their involvement in treatment. Representative strategies, as described by Miller and Rollnick (2002), include providing nonjudgmental feedback, giving advice regarding making change, decreasing the perceived desirability of alcohol misuse, expressing empathy, working to remove obstacles to change, and providing choices. These are described in detail in Chapter 4.

3.3.6   Self-Efficacy

In the context of treatment for AUDs, self-efficacy generally refers to the degree of confidence a patient has in his or her ability to avoid drinking (or to drink in moderation). It is most useful to assess self-efficacy not globally, but instead in the context of the various situations and environments in which

Clinical Pearl
Four Types of Situations Relevant to Self-Efficacy

- Situations involving negative affect, whether it be intrapersonal (e.g., feeling depressed) or interpersonal (e.g., feeling angry or frustrated).
- Situations involving social interactions (e.g., when offered a drink at a party) or positive emotions (e.g., when feeling excited).
- Situations involving physical and other concerns (e.g., when feeling physical discomfort or when feeling concerned about someone).
- Situations involving withdrawal and/or urges to drink.

From DiClemente et al. (1994)

the patient most often drinks. A starting point for this assessment is provided in the work of DiClemente, Carbonari, Montgomery, and Hughes (1994), who assessed alcohol patients' perceived confidence to avoid drinking in a variety of situations. They identified four domains of especially relevant situations (detailed in the box below). Other situations to assess likely will be generated by the patient when describing his or her current or recent drinking situations.

Clinicians may find it helpful to use standardized measures to assess self-efficacy for abstaining (or for avoiding heavy drinking) across a range of drinking situations. Such measures can be used at the beginning of treatment to help identify high-risk situations (described in detail in Section 3.3.8) as well as during treatment to monitor changes in self-efficacy. The Situational Confidence Questionnaire (SCQ; Annis, 1987), the SCQ–39 (Annis & Graham, 1988), and the 8-item Brief Situational Confidence Questionnaire (BSCQ; Breslin, Sobell, Sobell, & Agrawal, 2000) measure an individual's confidence in being able to *avoid heavy drinking*. The updated version of the SCQ, the Drug-Taking Confidence Questionnaire (DTCQ; Annis & Martin, 1985; Annis, Turner, & Sklar, 1997) is available for use at a nominal cost from the Centre for Addiction and Mental Health in Toronto, Ontario. The BSCQ is freely available for use and download from www.nova.edu/gsc. The Alcohol Abstinence Self-Efficacy Scale (AASE; DiClemente et al., 1994) measures temptation to drink and confidence to *abstain from drinking* across a variety of situations. The AASE is not copyrighted and there is no fee for use; we have included a copy of the AASE in the Appendix.

When measured at the beginning of treatment, higher self-efficacy for abstaining (or resisting heavy drinking) is associated consistently with better treatment outcomes and longer time to relapse. Although self-efficacy has been shown to increase over the course of treatment, changes in self-efficacy and end-of-treatment self-efficacy have been less consistently associated with outcome. These findings likely have two explanations. First, individuals who have the lowest self-efficacy at the beginning of treatment have the most room for improvement, yet they may have other poor prognostic factors. Second, in our clinical experience, self-efficacy at the end of treatment tends to be uniformly (and perhaps unrealistically) high, leaving little variance to predict outcome.

3.3.7   Coping Skills

Developing and utilizing coping skills is central to achieving and maintaining abstinence from alcohol

Possessing and effectively applying coping skills is central to maintaining abstinence from alcohol. In fact, Connors, Longabaugh, and Miller (1996), in summarizing a series of reports from a multisite study on relapse, found coping skills to be a particularly strong protective factor, whereas ineffective coping was a consistent predictor of relapse. Coping can be assessed globally (i.e., how well does the patient cope with what he or she faces as part of day-to-day life) as well as in the context of situations that pose risk for heavy drinking. *Coping also can be evaluated in terms of both emotional and behavioral skills.* Two useful self-report measures of global coping skills are the Ways of Coping Questionnaire (WCQ; Folkman & Lazarus, 1988) and the Coping Responses Inventory (CRI; Moos, 1995). Both measures are useful for identifying cognitive and behavioral coping strategies and deficits and for monitoring coping changes over time; both require an administration fee. As a means of assessing coping specific to alcohol use, the Coping Behaviors Inventory (CBI; Litman, Stapleton, Oppenheim, & Peleg, 1983) can be used to have patients rate how frequently they use a variety of strategies to refrain from drinking. The CBI can be used in conjunction with the Effectiveness of Coping Behaviors Inventory (ECBI; Litman, Stapleton, Oppenheim, Peleg, & Jackson, 1984), which allows patients to rate the same items in terms of how well these strategies have worked for them in the past. The Substance Abuse Relapse Assessment (Schonfeld, Peters, & Dolente, 1993) is a semistructured interview that allows the clinician to collect detailed, individualized information to identify high-risk situations and coping skills deficits. This strategy is similar to functional analysis, which will be discussed in detail in the next section.

3.3.8   High-Risk for Drinking Situations

Following the initiation of abstinence, patients are likely to face stressful situations that place them at risk for again using alcohol. These high-risk situations are a central component of the Marlatt model of relapse (Marlatt & Witkiewitz, 2005). Marlatt and his colleagues hypothesized that the establishment of abstinence from alcohol engenders a sense of personal control and self-efficacy. These self-perceptions become strengthened as the period of abstinence lengthens. When high-risk for drinking situations present themselves, the ideal response would be an effective coping behavior. When such a behavior is in the person's behavioral repertoire and is used, then the success experience is said to enhance the person's self-efficacy, as described earlier. This, in turn, is expected to decrease the probability of drinking in similar subsequent situations. On the other hand, if an individual in recovery from alcohol problems is unable to apply an effective self-management/coping response, then this will lead to a decreased level of self-efficacy and an increase in the attractiveness of alcohol as a mechanism for dealing with the situation. This is particularly the case if the person maintains positive outcome expectancies regarding alcohol effects. As the attractiveness of alcohol increases (in conjunction with decreased self-efficacy), it becomes more likely that the person will use alcohol in that situation. In decisional balance terms, this scenario represents a situation where the advantages of alcohol use again outweigh the advantages of abstinence.

In the early development of this model of relapse, Marlatt and Gordon (1980) interviewed individuals following treatment for alcohol use disorders to identify factors associated with returns to drinking. They identified two broad categories. The first represented intrapersonal-environmental stressors, which include determinants associated primarily with within-person factors and/or reactions to nonpersonal environmental events. Respondents identified intrapersonal-environmental stressors as accounting for 61% of relapse episodes. The five subcategories of intrapersonal-environmental stressors

Clinical Vignette
Sample Daily Drinking Diary and Discussion

Date and Time	Situation (e.g., where, who you are with, thoughts, moods, etc.)	Amount Consumed (type of beverages and number of standard drinks)	Consequences (e.g., positive or negative outcomes, thoughts, moods, etc.)
Friday 9/15/06 6–9 pm	Joe's Bar and Grill – happy hour after work with friends, celebrating coworker's promotion. Happy mood!	6 beers 2 tequila shots	Still happy afterward, wanted to continue drinking when I got home.
Friday 9/15/06 9 pm to midnight	At home, alone, watching TV. Still happy, feeling buzzed.	6 beers	Didn't sleep well, hung over the next morning.
Saturday 9/16/06 8–11 pm	Home, alone, watching football. No particular mood. Thinking I was stupid to have drank so much last night.	5 beers	None.
Sunday 9/17/06 4–10 pm	Friend's house, watching football. Happy mood.	12 beers	Sluggish the next morning, but not really hung over.

Discussion of Daily Drinking Diary

Therapist: So, how did it go filling out the self-monitoring log?
Patient: Well, it made me think more about my drinking, and I might have drunk a little less because I knew that we would be going over it together.
Therapist: I noticed that you wrote that you thought that you drank too much on Friday evening.
Patient: I had 14 drinks, and the drinks at the bar weren't cheap!
Therapist: So, you were upset about how much you spent?
Patient: That and how I felt the next day.
Therapist: How you felt?
Patient: Yeah. Pretty lousy. So I drank less on Saturday.

were coping with negative emotional states (38% of relapse episodes), coping with negative physical-physiological states (3%), enhancement of positive emotional states (this category was associated with relapse to other substance use, but not relapse to drinking), testing personal control (9%), or giving in to temptations or urges (11%). The second broad category represented interpersonal stressors, which include factors associated with interpersonal events. Interpersonal stressors were identified as accounting for 39% of all relapse episodes. The subcategories within this group were coping with interpersonal conflict (18% of relapse episodes), social pressure (18%), and enhancement of positive emotional states (3%). In sum, the majority of respondents attributed their relapse to intrapersonal stressors, and within that domain predominantly to negative emotional states.

Identifying high-risk situations for drinking

In clinical practice, it is useful to work with patients to identify their individual *high-risk situations for drinking*. This type of detailed assessment is often called *functional analysis*, and is discussed again in Chapter 4. Two sample handouts for this purpose (Daily Drinking Diary and Worksheet for Functional Analysis of Drinking Behavior) are provided in the Appendix. The Daily Drinking Diary is intended to be completed on a daily basis at home by the patient, whereas the Worksheet can be filled out in session to reflect past drinking episodes. As an interrelated aspect of completing a functional analysis, it is often useful to have patients identify coping skills they apply to avoid these situations or to otherwise deal with them when in the midst of them. A sample Daily Drinking Diary is provided above, followed by a hypothetical clinical dialogue discussing the diary in session.

3.3.9   Spirituality and Religiosity

Recent years have witnessed a growing appreciation for the role of spirituality and religiosity in the recovery process. Indeed, problems with alcohol have sometimes been called a "spiritual disease," and research has shown an inverse relationship between spirituality/religiosity and alcohol/drug use. Accordingly, patients should be asked about the role, or potential role, of spirituality and/or religiosity in their lives. For those patients providing an endorsement, spiritual and/or religious pursuits may contribute to the recovery process.

3.3.10   Previous Treatment Experiences

There will be considerable variation in the nature and frequency of previous treatment experiences. For several reasons, it will be important to assess these previous episodes. First, this information may provide insights on what treatment modalities have been associated with positive outcomes, such as an extended period of alcohol abstinence. Similarly, the clinician can garner insight on treatment approaches that have not yielded success. Second, the previous treatment history can be used as a starting point for understanding the time-course of previous treatments. For example, if previous treatments have been associated with certain periods of abstinence (e.g., six months), followed by a relapse, then a treatment focus, beyond reestablishing abstinence, would be relapse prevention and aftercare at least through the time point of previous relapses. Finally, the treatment history information may provide insights into why previous treatment initiatives have not succeeded.

3.3.11   Previous Self-Help Group Involvement

Many individuals entering treatment have previously attended self-help groups, most typically Alcoholics Anonymous (AA). It is worthwhile to assess any such involvement and to have patients describe their experiences, whether positive or negative. For patients with positive previous experiences, it would make sense for them to reinstate that involvement. For patients without previous AA exposure, or who hold negative views in the absence of previous exposure, it often is helpful to encourage attendance at several meetings in order to obtain that experience (see Self-Help Contract).

Patients should determine if self-help group involvement may be of benefit to them

---

Clinical Pearl
Self-Help Contract

In our own clinical work, we often contract with patients to attend four or so meetings within the next month and have them identify ways in which AA attendance may be of benefit to them in achieving and maintaining abstinence. This strategy is especially helpful with patients who are resistant to AA attendance because it allows them to experience the meetings in a finite, time-limited manner, with the option to continue their attendance if they find the meetings helpful.

3.3.12   Barriers to Treatment Participation

Another assessment domain is barriers to participation in treatment. It is unfortunately the case that a significant number of patients who initiate treatment do not follow through with treatment. This is particularly a problem among outpatients, with some studies indicating premature treatment termination rates exceeding 50%. One response to this problem is to engage patients at the beginning of the treatment endeavor, as discussed earlier in the context of facilitating motivational readiness to change. In addition, it is important to work with the patient to identify obstacles to treatment participation. These include treatment costs, transportation costs or availability, lost time from work, and child care or family responsibilities. Once potential obstacles are identified, the therapist and patient can collaborate on problem solving as many of these obstacles as possible.

3.4   Life-Functioning

Considerable attention has been devoted to assessment of drinking history and domains with particular relevance to alcohol consumption. In accordance with the biopsychosocial model of AUDs discussed in Chapter 2, we believe that it is important to assess other areas of life-functioning in addition to alcohol consumption. Key areas might include (but are not limited to) psychological functioning, interpersonal functioning, physical health, quality of life, social functioning, stress, financial issues, work-related issues, and significant life events. We review a few of the major such domains below, recognizing that functioning in these areas may be related directly to the extent of the alcohol use disorder. For readers seeking more detailed information on assessment of alcohol involvement and other domains of life-functioning, there are a number of excellent resources that offer comprehensive presentations of a host of assessment measures (Allen & Wilson, 2003; Donovan & Marlatt, 2005; Rush et al., 2000).

Assessing other domains of overall life-functioning

One high-priority domain warranting evaluation is *psychological functioning*. Within this context, the therapist should observe the patient's affect and inquire about the patient's mood, noting any history of mood disturbances and treatment. In addition, the therapist will want to assess general cognitive functioning, suicidal ideation, and thoughts of harming others.

A second domain of clinical interest is the patient's *interpersonal functioning*, especially with family and with friends. These individuals may be useful adjuncts to the treatment course. It will be useful as well to assess the patient's social network more broadly to identify social supports and anchors.

Finally, it is important to assess *physical health*. Although it may be wise to refer all patients for a general physical examination, this is particularly the case among patients describing physical complaints. The physical examination typically includes a laboratory workup. Blood tests, for example, can provide useful information generally, but particularly in the context of recent heavy alcohol consumption. Typically this involves examination of certain liver enzymes, such as aspartate aminotransferase (AST), alanine aminotransferase (ALT), and gamma-glutamyl-transferase (GGT), which tend to be most reactive to recent heavy drinking. Although these tests are by no means perfect indicators of the level of alcohol use, elevated liver enzymes suggest the need to probe further about heavy alcohol use in the context of a more comprehensive assessment. In addition, abnormal laboratory values may suggest a medical problem that is either caused or worsened by heavy alcohol use (Allen, Sillanaukee, Strid, & Litten, 2003). Laboratory tests should only be used as a screening measure; normal values do not rule out the possibility of recent heavy alcohol use (Sobell, Agrawal, & Sobell, 1999). Urinalysis can be arranged for purposes of screening for recent drug use.

3.5   Prioritizing Problems and Needs

Once the initial assessment process has been completed, the therapist and patient are in a position to organize the available data, to identify treatment goals, and to prioritize those goals. All of this results in the treatment plan, which is described in the following section. After that, we discuss considerations in the evaluation of treatment indications.

3.5.1 Developing the Treatment Plan

The treatment plan is the culmination of the assessment process. Treatment goals are identified and prioritized. As with the assessment process more generally, the development of the treatment process should be collaborative in nature, reflecting the inputs of both the therapist and patient. Treatment goals should be reasonably specific and also achievable.

Treatment goals should be specific and achievable

In addition to the above, *it is important that the treatment plan be highly individualized*, and thus incorporate consideration of the patient's unique history, circumstances, and social and psychological strengths and resources. Further, the treatment plan should be viewed as a starting point for behavior change in one or more domains. As such, it should be viewed as a document that can be revised as progress is made or as new issues emerge.

3.5.2 Treatment Indications

The development of the treatment plan sets the stage for the identification and evaluation of potential treatment indications for each treatment goal. In cases where alcohol dependence is the presenting concern, achieving and maintaining abstinence typically will be the highest priority, and treatment strategies designed to produce abstinence will be applied. A goal of drinking moderation might be appropriate for individuals who are not severely physically dependent on alcohol and who express a preference for reducing their drinking to nonproblem levels. Furthermore, because significant decreases in drinking can result in marked improvements in patients' health and general well-being, sometimes drinking reduction can be established as a reasonable interim goal for patients who are resistant to abstaining from alcohol, and the need for complete abstinence can be reevaluated at a later point in the treatment. The important point is to identify and prioritize treatment goals so that the most effective and efficient interventions can be matched to these goals.

3.6 Referral Issues

Alcohol abuse is almost always associated with dysfunction in other areas of life, such as marital, family, vocational, mental health, and/or physical health. These potential problem areas, which will have been identified in the assessment phase, will need to be addressed as well in the treatment plan process, although some of these difficulties may dissipate with the establishment of abstinence or a significant reduction in drinking. Problems in some areas likely can and will be addressed within the sessions with the therapist. Others, however, may require consultation or referral for adjunct treatment. An example would be medical problems that should be addressed by the patient's physician. Another example would be referral to a psychiatrist for evaluation for pharmacotherapy for an affective disorder or for use of medication to reduce craving. Maintaining a listing of reliable referral sources for different types of problems will allow the therapist to be prepared for these scenarios.

4

Treatment

4.1 Introduction and Overview

This chapter covers several different questions about empirically supported AUD treatments. We first consider the main part of this chapter, which is a description of the treatment methods themselves that have been identified as "empirically supported." As part of our description of each treatment method, we also discuss hypothesized mechanisms of action for the different treatments and any research relevant to those hypotheses. The next section of the chapter considers the degree of efficacy or effectiveness that each treatment method has shown in empirical studies. The last two sections of the chapter concern possible variations in administering the treatments in question, and any problems in implementing them, respectively.

4.1.1 Meaning of Empirically Supported

Before proceeding with this chapter it is important first to address what is meant by the term "empirically supported" and its implications for application of a given treatment method. Since Guyatt (1992) argued for the need to practice "evidence based medicine," whether a treatment (medical or psychological) is empirically supported has been an essential and controversial question. (Alternative terms that have been used are "empirically validated" or "evidence based;"; Levant, 2004). In a nutshell, the term empirically supported as used in this book refers to the research evidence that supports the efficacy or effectiveness of a given treatment method. Empirical evidence is only one of at least three dimensions that must be considered in deciding whether to apply a treatment method.

The importance of applying treatment methods that are empirically supported

Saying that "empirically supported" refers to research evidence still is not specific enough, as there are countless data that may qualify as research evidence. Therefore, it also is important to specify what schema is being used to determine whether a treatment method is classified as empirically supported. In this chapter we follow the summaries of the literature on empirically supported treatments for the substance use disorders provided by McGovern and Carroll (2003) and McGovern, Fox, Xie, and Drake (2004) in determining what behavioral/psychological therapies and pharmacotherapies to list as empirically supported. All of these treatment methods may be viewed as having at least some empirical support for the modification of patterns of alcohol use, but some have stronger support than others. Interested readers may consult McGovern and Carroll for full details.

It is important to note that the inclusion of specific treatment methods in this chapter should not be construed as a recommendation to use any one of them with a specific patient in a given setting. In this regard, we agree with the Institute of Medicine's (2001) argument that application of a treatment method depends not only on the scientific evidence for its effectiveness, but also on patient values (for example, expectations about treatment content, patient preferences), patient resources (time willing to spend on treatment, finances to pay for it), and context (for example, provider skills, expense, time available). Note that this approach also is consistent with the biopsychosocial model's approach to selection of treatment that was discussed in Chapter 2 and with assessment and treatment decision making approaches that were discussed in Chapter 3.

4.1.2   Self-Help/Mutual-Help Groups

This chapter also considers the use of self-help and mutual help groups, but separately from the other treatment methods. The reason for considering self-help methods separately is that they technically are not "professionally" developed or administered. Rather, they are peer-led. In addition, because of their philosophical basis, 12-step programs have rarely been evaluated by use of randomized clinical trials. On the other hand, there is a considerable amount of observational data on self-help groups (particularly 12-step programs) that have accumulated and that offer evidence about their effectiveness (Humphreys et al., 2004). Such data, and the high degree of popularity of self-help groups, warrant their inclusion here.

4.2   Behavioral and Psychological Methods

This section includes several treatment methods that have empirical support for (primarily) efficacy in the treatment of high-risk (for the development or presence) of alcohol problems or AUDs. The methods are brief interventions (BIs), motivational interviewing (MI) and motivational enhancement (ME), and cognitive behavior therapy (CBT). In subsequent sections, we discuss several extensions of CBT (behavioral couples' therapy, contingency management and community reinforcement, and relapse prevention) and pharmacotherapy.

4.2.1   Brief Interventions (BIs)

Definition
"Brief intervention" does not refer to a single entity but to a collection of interventions. As the name implies, BIs are limited in the time that they take to deliver, as compared to traditional treatments. For example, one earlier paper (Babor, 1994) suggested that BIs range in time from one 5-minute session of advice, to as much as three one-hour sessions. However, the vast majority of

them are less than 25 minutes long, consisting of one session with one or more brief follow-up contacts. The initial session(s) of BIs have been delivered in person, by computer, or by telephone, or some combination of those methods. Follow-up contacts typically are not in person, but by telephone.

BIs for alcohol use probably have their most direct connection with adaptation of a public health model for the use of BIs for the modification of cigarette smoking in the primary care and other medical settings, an approach that has proved to be successful. In the early 1980s this approach began to be applied to patterns of alcohol use, particularly in Western Europe, as publications of alcohol BIs began to appear in the scientific literature. This trend became evident in the United States in the later 1980s and has burgeoned since then.

Brief interventions are often used with "at-risk" drinkers who typically are not alcohol-dependent

Alcohol BIs are not only distinguished by the time that they take to administer, but also by the primary patient populations that they target. BIs have been evaluated primarily with individuals who are not physically dependent on alcohol (Whitlock, Polen, Green, Orleans, & Klein, 2004). When we say that there is empirical support for alcohol BIs, that conclusion refers to nonalcohol dependent individuals. Using a public health approach, clinical researchers have tested BIs primarily in settings where individuals present for health problems *other than* their alcohol use, such as in primary medical care settings or in emergency departments. There is no a priori reason for confining the application of BIs to these settings, but the "full population" approach to treatment that BIs represent commonly finds their implementation there. It also is notable that primary and other medical care settings are good places to implement alcohol BIs, as individuals who present in these settings have a disproportionately high rate of at risk or problem alcohol use, because of the association of such use with various physical problems.

In the same way, there is no current empirical evidence to show that BIs are *not* efficacious or effective when used with alcohol dependent patients. Nevertheless, at least in the published literature, we see little evaluation of alcohol BIs with *dependent* patients as a "stand alone" treatment (that is, when the BI is the entire intervention and is not used as a way to encourage the patient to engage in more intensive, specialized alcohol treatment). This may be due to several factors, one of which is clinical guidelines. For example, the U.S. Department of Veterans Affairs guidelines for treatment of alcohol use and related problems include recommendations to refer those individuals who are assessed as alcohol dependent to "specialized" treatment settings. Alcohol BIs are considered only for individuals who are not dependent. Besides the family of BIs considered here and motivational interviewing (which also may be considered a BI and is described next), the treatment methods that are described in this chapter are considered to be applicable and empirically supported for individuals who are diagnosed with alcohol abuse or dependence.

Goals of BIs

The primary goal of brief interventions is to reduce alcohol consumption to below "risk" levels

In the case of alcohol use, the primary goal of BIs is to help the individual reduce his or her level of alcohol consumption to below "risk" (for alcohol-related problems) levels. What is "at risk" drinking? The threshold for at risk drinking has been defined in different ways in different parts of the world. The definition that has been used by the U.S. National Institute on Alcohol Abuse and Alcoholism (NIAAA, an Institute of the U.S. National Institutes of Health) and that is widely used in research and clinical practice in the United States is, for one day, no more than four standard drinks (SDs) for men, and no more than three SDs for women. The cut off for a week is no more than 14 SDs for men up to 65 years of age, and no more than seven SDs for women and for men older than 65. As we noted in Chapter 3, a SD is the beverage alcohol equivalent of 0.6 ounces of ethanol (as contained in 12 ounces of 5% alcohol beer, 5 ounces of 12% alcohol table wine, or 1.5 ounces of 40% alcohol hard liquor). NIAAA (2007) also offers guidelines for what is considered to be a "safe level of drinking," which is defined as a level that causes "few if any problems." Specifically, the safe drinking guidelines suggest no more than two standard drinks per day for men and no more than one drink per day for women and older adults. Note that both sets of guidelines are general; what is "at risk" may vary from person to person based on factors such as comorbidity (psychiatric or medical), undergoing pharmacotherapy for another problem that might interact negatively with alcohol (or another drug), or pregnancy in women. It is interesting to note that there is a gap between the level of drinking that is considered "at risk" and amounts considered "safe." Specific decisions about goals for drinking reduction should be arrived at based on individual patient circumstances.

Mechanisms of Action

BIs have been thought to produce their effects by advancing an individual's readiness to change a problem behavior, which in turn motivates the application of "inherent" coping and other behavioral skills that create behavior change. Although there is no direct empirical support for this hypothesized mechanism of change, a meta-analysis on the efficacy of alcohol BIs published by Bien, Miller, and Tonigan (1993) concluded that at least two of six elements were present in efficacious alcohol BIs. The six elements are identified by the acronym FRAMES and are described in the Clinical Pearl below (FRAMES will be discussed in greater detail later in the chapter).

Other reviews of alcohol brief interventions have appeared in the literature, and they have derived an algorithm of sorts that represents the "common

---

Clinical Pearl
FRAMES – Effective Elements of Alcohol Brief Interventions

F = Feedback	Provide feedback about alcohol use and emphasize potential risks.
R = Responsibility	Emphasize patient's choice and responsibility regarding change.
A = Advice	Offer specific advice regarding amount of change that is indicated.
M = Menu	Provide a menu of options for making changes.
E = Empathy	Demonstrate sensitivity for the patient's thoughts and feelings.
S = Self-Efficacy	Instill confidence that the patient can make recommended changes.

Clinical Pearl
Five As – Common Elements of Alcohol Brief Interventions

1. **Ask** – Ask patient about alcohol use.

2. **Assess** – Determine whether patient meets criteria for alcohol abuse or dependence diagnosis.

3. **Advise** – Offer feedback about patient's alcohol consumption and provide advice suggesting that patient quit or reduce drinking.

4. **Assist** – Determine patient's level of readiness for change and offer appropriate help concerning setting goals for change.

5. **Arrange** – Arrange for follow-up contacts if indicated.

Clinical Pearl
Relevant Settings for Brief Interventions

- Primary care offices and medical clinics
- Mental health clinics
- Specialty medical settings
- Detoxification centers
- Emergency rooms

elements" of alcohol BIs. One example is the "Five As" (see Clinical Pearl) represented in the NIAAA *Clinician's Guide* (2005). As we will see, not surprisingly, several of these resemble the FRAMES elements. The Five As are designed to be administered in person, which is by far the most common way to deliver alcohol BIs. In addition, because alcohol BIs so often are delivered in contexts such as primary care, the guide is targeted to primary care providers. We discuss the algorithm presented in the guide from that perspective, although the steps described in working with patients could be applied easily in other healthcare contexts as well.

Implementation of Brief Interventions in Medical Settings

The first step in the "Five As" BI process (*Ask*) involves identifying individuals who are candidates for alcohol BIs. This step typically involves using one of the several excellent brief, self-report alcohol screening tools for adults that have been evaluated extensively. One such alcohol screening tool is the Alcohol Use Disorders Identification Test (AUDIT), which is reproduced as an Appendix in this volume. Providers need to decide who will administer the screen (the clinician, or other staff such as nurses or behavioral health consultants) and what patients to target for screening. For example, a practice may decide to screen all new patients presenting for services (and perhaps do so annually) or to screen high-risk groups, such as smokers, pregnant women, and young adults (age 18–30). Once a screening system is organized patients can be identified as candidates for alcohol BIs.

Patients first are asked if they consume beverages that contain alcohol. If the answer is "no," then the screening is complete. If the answer is "yes," then

The AUDIT is a brief screening tool for identifying problem drinkers

the patient is either asked if he or she had any heavy "risk" drinking days (as defined earlier) in the past year, or is asked to complete a standardized screen, such as the AUDIT. If the patient is asked but reports no heavy drinking days in the last year, then the provider advises him or her about the definition of daily and weekly limits of "risk" drinking for the patient's sex and age group, recommends lower limits of alcohol use, including abstinence, if medically indicated, and informs the patient that the provider is open to discussing alcohol use at any time. The NIAAA guidelines recommend alcohol screening annually and more often if indicated.

Providers have the option of not asking about heavy drinking, but instead asking the patient to complete a standardized screen such as the AUDIT. If that is the case, and the patient scores negative on the screen, then the patient is given the same advice and information as that received by patients who reported no heavy drinking days. The NIAAA Guide gives the option of using the heavy drinking question alone as a screen; however, that course should be taken with caution, as it could lead to many "false positive" cases, that is, a screen that is highly sensitive but not specific (for high-risk or problem drinking).

If the patient is positive on whatever screening option is used, then the NIAAA suggests first asking the patient the number of days a week he or she drinks alcohol on average, and the number of risky or heavy drinking days a week that are typical. The patient's responses are recorded in the patient's record as "preintervention" level of alcohol consumption. The next stage of the algorithm, *Assess*, begins by evaluating whether the patient has current (last 12 months) "alcohol use disorder," as defined formally by an established nomenclature such as the DSM or ICD (see Chapter 1). This is done by use of a simple checklist of symptoms that constitute alcohol abuse or alcohol dependence according to the diagnostic system that is followed. Therefore, for example, if DSM-IV-TR is followed, then the patient is asked whether his or her drinking repeatedly caused or contributed to any of the following symptoms in the last 12 months: role failure (interference with home, work, or school obligations), risk of bodily harm (drinking and driving, operating machinery, swimming), run-ins with the law (arrests or other legal problems), or relationship trouble (family, friends). It is evident that these symptoms are the DSM "abuse" criteria. In the same way, the patient is asked questions to determine if he or she is positive for alcohol dependence. If the patient does not meet criteria for an AUD, then the assessment defines him or her as "at risk" for developing one based on the positive initial screen. If the patient does meet criteria for abuse or dependence, then he or she is designated as having a current AUD. This completes the *Assess* step, and the process now moves to *Advise and Assist*.

If the assessment phase identifies the patient as an "at risk" drinker, *Advise and Assist* proceeds as follows. First, the conclusion of the assessment is reviewed with the patient, including the information that he or she is drinking more than is safe medically. For this purpose, the patient might be shown a pie chart that illustrates how common (or, more to the point, unusual) his or her drinking quantity and frequency is in the population of men or women, as relevant. This is a form of *feedback* to the patient. We have provided gender specific pie charts in the Appendix that can be used for this purpose. The patient then is given *advice* regarding his or her drinking, such as to quit entirely or to reduce drinking to below risk levels. For the at-risk drinker, common reasons for advising abstinence from alcohol are medical or psychiatric contraindications to alcohol use, taking medications that interact with alcohol, and pregnancy or plans to become pregnant. NIAAA notes other considerations, such as a family history of AUDs, advanced age, and injuries related to drinking. While providing feedback and advice, the clinician should take the opportunity to discuss the medical risks of heavy drinking. We offer an example of providing such feedback in the vignette below.

Once advice about a drinking goal is articulated, then the provider briefly assesses the patient's readiness to change his or her alcohol use patterns. Along these lines, the provider simply asks, "Are you willing to consider making changes in your drinking?" Based on the patient's response, the provider decides whether the patient is ready to commit to make changes in his or her alcohol use. If the provider decides that the patient does not seem committed to changing his or her alcohol use at the present time, the provider restates his or her concern about the patient's health, encourages the patient to reflect what he or she likes about drinking at current levels compared to the reasons for reducing it, and to think about any major impediments or barriers to change. The provider also reaffirms his or her availability for helping the patient make

---

Clinical Vignette

Providing Feedback Regarding Hazardous Drinking

Therapist: Let's take a look at how your drinking compares to other men in the U.S. First of all, you can see from this pie chart that about 42% of men did not consume any alcohol in the past month. Your drinking falls into this small wedge here. Only about 10% of men drink five or more drinks on the same occasion on five or more days in a given month. Would you have guessed that the amount you drink ranks in the highest 10%?

Patient: No, I had no idea. I usually think of myself as an average drinker. Although my wife is often getting on my case about how much I drink.

Therapist: The other thing to consider is how your drinking may affect your health, either currently or in the long term. As I mentioned before, the recommendations of the National Institutes of Health show that for men who are otherwise healthy, drinking five or more drinks on any given day is associated with increased risk. Although most people know that heavy drinking can eventually cause liver problems, many people aren't aware of the other potential medical risks that go along with heavy drinking. For example, heavy drinkers are at increased risk for heart disease, high blood pressure, many types of cancer, and some types of stroke. Alcohol can also make existing medical conditions worse, and it can interact with many types of medication. That's not to mention the increased risk of accidental injury while drinking and of course the risks associated with driving while under the influence.

Patient: That's a lot of risks.

Therapist: I know it's a lot of information to take in all at once. I'm going to give you a booklet to take home that has more information on some of these risks. Maybe we can talk about whether you're ready to make some changes. What do you think?

changes when ready. Therefore, for patients who do not seem to be ready to make changes in their alcohol use, *Assist* consists of encouraging the patient to consider changing and the benefits of doing so vs. the benefits of making no changes. The provider also makes clear that he or she is available whenever the *patient* determines that he or she is ready to make changes.

If the provider decides that the patient is ready to make changes in his or her alcohol use, the patient is encouraged to set a goal for change, such as to reduce use to below the relevant risk levels for that person. The provider then helps the patient develop a plan for change, which might include the steps that will be taken to facilitate change, such as avoiding a favorite bar or associating with heavy drinking friends, how the patient plans to monitor his or her drinking, how "high-risk" situations will be managed (similar to the first action step, these are ways that the individual will handle being in situations that have been associated in the past with frequent heavy or problem alcohol use), and the provision of educational materials. The latter is one of the several descriptions of the "facts on alcohol" that often are presented in pamphlet format and that are available from sources such as NIAAA and the World Health Organization. In summary, the *Assist* stage for patients who are ready to make changes in their drinking consists of helping patients define goals for change and specific ways to reach them and to monitor their progress toward doing so. In Table 7 below we have presented a hypothetical example of goals for drinking reduction (to nonhazardous levels) or abstinence for a male patient who presented to the brief intervention reporting that he drinks on average 27 drinks per week and that he often has as many as 9 drinks on a given drinking occasion.

The NIAAA guide does not call the follow-up phase *Arrange*, but this designation has appeared in the literature. It simply means that the last part of the

Table 7
Hypothetical Example of Goals for Drinking Reduction

Hypothetical Goals for Reduction	Hypothetical Goals for Abstinence
I will not go to bars more than one night per week.	I will not go to any of my usual drinking hang-outs (bar, Jim's house, bowling alley).
When I am drinking, I will alternate between alcoholic drinks and soft drinks.	When I am out with friends, I will only drink soft drinks.
When I am drinking an alcoholic beverage, I will take small sips (never gulp!). I will not drink more than one drink per hour.	I will tell my spouse and my friends that I am trying to quit drinking, so that they can help me if I am feeling tempted.
I will not drink more than two drinks containing alcohol on any given day.	I will attend at least two AA meetings per week.
If I feel tempted to drink too much, I will try to distract myself with other activities, such as talking to a friend.	I will try to do something fun (such as tennis or bike riding) to reward myself on every day that I don't drink.

clinical algorithm is to *arrange* for follow-up contacts with the patient. The main purpose of these one or more contacts is to evaluate alcohol use since the last contact and to discuss progress toward reaching the change goal(s) that were specified at the initial BI session. If the patient is found to have reached his or her designated goal(s) and has sustained it, then the provider reinforces and supports continued adherence. There also is a reevaluation of drinking goals if that is relevant, and an effort to encourage the patient to contact the provider if maintaining change becomes difficult or is no longer working. In addition, as noted earlier, the provider should continue to screen the patient at least annually.

If the at risk patient at follow-up is discovered not to have achieved the desired goal or has not maintained the changes achieved, then the provider acknowledges to the patient that change is indeed difficult. At the same time, the provider supports any progress toward goal achievement that the patient does report. In addition, failure to reduce alcohol use successfully may indicate the utility of implementing a trial abstinence period, considering engaging significant others (spouse or close friends, for example), and reassessing the patient for the presence of an AUD.

If the *Assess* step suggests that the patient has a current AUD, then the *Advise and Assist* steps proceed as follows. The provider first states his or her conclusion and recommendations clearly. For example, the provider might say, "Based on the information about your alcohol use patterns that you reported today, it is likely that you may have an alcohol use disorder, and we recommend that you stop drinking" (the latter alternative is still thought by many in clinical settings to be the safest option for patients with AUDs). The provider also relates the possible AUD to the patient's health or other concerns. This feedback is followed by the negotiation of a drinking goal with the patient; again, abstinence is the preferred option. However, if the patient will not accept abstinence, and especially if abuse or dependence is not judged to be severe, then the patient may be able to moderate consumption successfully, and the designation of the drinking goal may proceed as described for "at risk," non-AUD patients. Third, especially if the patient is alcohol dependent, then referral to specialized alcohol treatment should be considered. In the same vein, mutual self-help group (described later in this chapter) involvement might be an option. Furthermore, for alcohol dependent patients, medication for alcohol withdrawal might be necessary, and medication as part of the treatment for alcohol dependence (such AUD pharmacotherapy is described later in this chapter) might be useful. Finally, a follow-up contact should be arranged.

As described for the at-risk drinker, follow-up contacts focus on the patient's achievement and maintenance of the drinking goal. If the goal has been achieved and maintained, then the provider reinforces and supports continued adherence to the recommended changes. If an addiction specialist now is treating the patient, the provider should coordinate care with that individual. Finally, any co-occurring medical or psychiatric problems should be addressed as necessary.

If the follow-up contact reveals that the patient has not reached or maintained his or her goal, then the steps indicated begin with the provider's acknowledgement that change is difficult. Also similar to working with at-risk drinkers, the provider supports any movement toward change that was achieved. Once again, if relevant, the provider connects the patient's alcohol use to problems in other areas (legal, social, work) as relevant. If these steps have not been taken already, the provider considers referral to an alcohol treatment specialist, mutual self-help group involvement, engaging significant others, and presenting medication for patients who are alcohol dependent. Finally, co-occurring medical or psychiatric disorders are addressed as necessary.

General Points about Interacting with Patients in BI Delivery

Consistent with the FRAMES elements cited earlier, there are additional points about the style of interacting with patients while implementing alcohol BIs that are critical. First, the provider takes an objective, nonjudgmental approach in talking to the patient, and educational materials typically are provided as part of the intervention. Second, BIs are "patient centered," that is, the provider does not dictate the course of change, but the patient does. Change is viewed as emanating from within the patient; we will see this emphasis in full in discussion of our next treatment method, motivational interviewing/motivational enhancement. Third, the provider places responsibility for change on the patient. And last, the provider reaffirms the patient's ability (self-efficacy) to make the changes in alcohol use that are desired.

Brief interventions are patient-centered, nonjudgmental, and often educational in nature

4.2.2   Motivational Interviewing (MI)/Motivational Enhancement (ME)

General Background and Mechanisms

Our discussion of MI/ME is based on a presentation by Carey and Maisto (2006). The bases of MI/ME are the work of psychologists William R. Miller and Stephen Rollnick and began to appear in the research and clinical literature over 20 years ago. This foundation of MI/ME is an integration of concepts from motivational psychology, social psychology, and the theory and practice of psychotherapy. It is important to note that MI is primarily a style of interacting with patients that also underlies ME; ME includes the addition of systematic feedback to the patient about his or her behavior, such as alcohol use, and its consequences. MI may be defined as "a patient centered, directive method for enhancing intrinsic motivation to change by exploring and resolving ambivalence" (Miller & Rollnick, 2002, p. 30). Here the premises of MI/ME may be distilled into four major points:

The core premises of motivational interviewing are four-fold

1. Individuals have the inner resources to change their own behavior.
2. Change can be initiated and sustained successfully by the individual if he or she becomes aware of the benefits of changing and of the disadvantages of not changing (i.e., if the individual becomes "motivated" to change).
3. The process of changing a behavior may be described by Prochaska and DiClemente's (Prochaska, DiClemente, & Norcross, 1992) stages of change model. The present version of the model includes five main stages, in the following sequence from not motivated to change to engaging in and sustaining change activities: precontemplation – contemplation – preparation – action – maintenance (see Clinical Pearl below). When individuals are in the precontemplation or contemplation

Clinical Pearl
Stages of Change

Precontemplation – Not actively acknowledging a problem or not intending to change.

Contemplation – Thinking about making a change, but not actively changing behavior.

Preparation – Intending to change; ready to take action.

Action – Actively making changes in behavior.

Maintenance – Sustaining change and/or avoiding return to prior problem behaviors.

stages regarding changing a problem behavior, the idea is to "bring" them to the determination or action stages, where their inner resources will take over and drive whatever behavior changes are required to meet the individual's goals. The stages of change model has intuitive appeal to clinicians, has helped to emphasize the relevance of motivation to successful treatment outcome, and has been influential in the development of treatment programs that are tailored to the needs of individual patients. However, like most models, some aspects of the SOC model have been criticized (e.g., Davidson, 1998; West, 2005). This includes concerns regarding the assessment of readiness to change in the context of discrete stages. It has been suggested that readiness is better viewed on a continuum, rather than as a component of discrete stage categories (e.g., Carey, Purnine, Maisto, & Carey, 1999; Sutton, 1996). The Readiness Ruler (provided and discussed in Chapter 3) is a practical tool for determining how to evaluate patients with regard to their current motivational readiness to change. Because the Readiness Ruler uses a continuous scale, it circumvents problems potentially associated with trying to categorize patients into distinct stages.

4. Clinicians are likely to encounter patients at varying levels of readiness to change with regard to their alcohol consumption. MI/ME may be thought of as a collection of techniques to initiate and accelerate the individual's progress along the continuum of readiness to change.

ME is also organized around components hypothesized to be part of effective alcohol brief interventions. As we reviewed earlier in this chapter, these active components have been summarized by the acronym *FRAMES*. *F* refers to giving the individual objective *f*eedback about his or her behavior in order to make salient to him or her the possible risks of continuing to engage in that behavior. *R* refers to *r*esponsibility, or to making it clear to the individual that it is his or her choice about whether to make a change and, if that choice is made, that the *r*esponsibility for change lies with the individual. *A* refers to *a*dvice, or to direct counseling about whether a change would be in the individual's best interests and, if so, what degree of change. *M* stands for *m*enu, which means that several options to make changes should be presented to the individual, and not just one. *E* refers to *e*mpathy, which refers loosely to the capacity to put oneself in another's place, resulting in being sensitive to his or her thoughts

Clinical Vignette
Use of the FRAMES Acronym in a Therapy Session

Therapist: Based on the results of your liver function tests, there seems to be some damage to your liver as a result of your drinking. (Feedback)

Patient: Wow. I never realized that I was drinking enough to jeopardize my health.

Therapist: Well, it's up to you what to do with this information, to think about whether you want to make some changes. (Responsibility)

Patient: I wouldn't even know where to start making changes. I've been drinking every day since I was in high school.

Therapist: There are several different things you could try. Different things work better for some people than others. You could try cutting back, or you could try stopping "cold turkey." You might think about changing some of the places where you spend time or changing some of the people you spend time with. (Menu)

Patient: I have damage to my liver and now I have to change everything. That's a lot to think about.

Therapist: It feels a little overwhelming to get this news about your health and to have to think about how you might make some big changes in your life. (Empathy)

Patient: I'm really worried that I won't be able to do it.

Therapist: I remember you telling me that you stopped smoking when you realized that you were feeling out of breath every time you played catch with your son. You had the motivation and the reason to change your smoking. You could probably use some of those same skills to work on your drinking. (Self-Efficacy)

Patient: That's true. Quitting smoking was one of the hardest things I ever did. But somehow I did it. And I haven't had a cigarette in almost three years.

and feelings. The technical application of empathy in ME is discussed in detail later. Finally, *S* stands for *s*elf-efficacy, or the instilling in the individual the belief that he or she has the capacity to make the changes that are desired.

MI/ME is a "brief" (relative to the duration of traditional alcohol treatment) intervention that consists of (a) building motivation to change, followed by (b) strengthening commitment to change. This discussion focuses on MI, as it is the sole or main (for ME) component of these motivational interventions.

MI may be described on three levels. The first is the "spirit" of MI, defined by its being collaborative, patient centered, and designed to work with patient ambivalence about change, which is seen not as pathological but as expected and a normal part of the process of change. Second, MI may be defined by five principles, which are express empathy, develop discrepancy, avoid argumentation, roll with resistance, and support self-efficacy. Third, MI may be defined as a series of techniques that are used to achieve its aims.

Spirit of MI

MI is a *collaborative* intervention. This means that the therapist works *with* the patient and does not do things *to* the patient. In addition, the therapist generally guides but does not direct the patient regarding change. Collaborative also means that the therapist encourages the patient to be an active rather than a passive participant in his or her change efforts. Finally, therapists do not tell

Appreciating the "spirit" of motivational interviewing is central to its application

their patients what their problem is, why they should care about changing it, or how to change it. These conclusions about the patient's changing his or her behavior should come from the patient instead.

MI is a *patient-centered* intervention. Following from the idea of collaboration, patient-centered means that the therapist seeks to learn what the patient wants to change and why. Moreover, the therapist needs to identify what the patient's goals are, not what some external standard thinks that they should be. In addition, any change plan that is developed needs to be tailored to the patient in question. That is, the therapist determines what would likely work best for a given patient and what change plan that patient will accept.

In MI the therapist *explores and resolves ambivalence*. Ambivalence means that the desire to change and the desire not to change a given behavior are roughly in equilibrium. In fact, the MI session may be seen to have the goal of tipping this balance in the favor of reasons to change. Therefore, what therapists often say is that a lack of motivation in their patients may be more productively construed as the pros and cons of changing being in balance. How the therapist responds to ambivalence may affect how the balance of pros and cons of change is altered. Indeed, an assumption of MI is that more confrontational interactions with patients (e.g., saying directly to them that they have a problem with alcohol and that it is time that it is faced) tend to tip the balance to the side of staying the same – i.e., to the side of no change.

Five Principles of MI

Five principles of motivational interviewing

The five principles of MI refer to ongoing guides for information exchange and general interaction with patients. They are express empathy, develop discrepancy, avoid argumentation, roll with resistance, and support self-efficacy.

Express empathy. Empathy ensures that MI is patient centered. Express empathy means that through his or her actions and interactions with the patient, the therapist shows awareness of where the patient is at the moment as to his or her thoughts and feelings about changing the behavior in question. The therapist does not try to push his or her agenda by interacting with the patient based on some prescribed or otherwise predetermined course for change, but rather attends to where the patient is at the moment and responds accordingly. Research has demonstrated that an empathic therapist style is likely to elicit acknowledgement of problems by the patient, whereas a confrontational therapist style is likely to elicit arguing with, interrupting, and ignoring the therapist (Miller, Benefield, & Tonigan, 1993). A clinical vignette is presented later in this chapter, demonstrating the use of empathy during a therapy session.

Develop discrepancy. The MI session works toward the patient's perception of the gap that may exist between stated goals or desired behaviors ("where I want to be") and the patient's actual behavior ("where I am"). The assumption is that, without such a perception of discrepancy, there would be little incentive for the patient to make a change in the target behavior.

Avoid argumentation. The therapist should avoid the temptation to insist that the patient needs to change, especially when the patient is showing ambivalence. All efforts to elicit change should be made as suggestions, rather than as commands. If the therapist becomes forceful or argumentative, the patient is likely to "push back" even harder against making changes.

Roll with resistance. This principle follows on the idea of avoiding argumentation and was referred to a few times earlier in discussion of other features of MI. It means that therapist-patient interactions are not confrontational or directive if the patient is showing ambivalence about making specific behavior changes or, more simply, in defining goals for change. Rather, the therapist uses reflection (discussed later as an MI technique) to help the patient explore his or her ambivalence and, through that process, come to recognize the decided benefits of change. In this way, the patient, and not the therapist, concludes that change is the correct course for the patient.

Support self-efficacy. This principle of MI means that in their interactions with patients, therapists encourage the belief that the patient is capable of making, or has the skills to make, the changes in behavior that he or she desires.

Perhaps more than any other treatment method described in this book, MI is defined by its suggested style or spirit of interacting with patients. It is likely that MI initially gained the widespread attention of alcohol clinicians and clinical researchers because it presented a clear alternative to the more traditional "therapist-centered," confrontational way of interacting with patients and to responding to patient ambivalence (or resistance) about change.

Techniques of MI

As with any treatment method, MI consists of techniques, or actions, that therapists take to achieve the aims of the treatment. For MI, these techniques focus on ways therapists initiate conversations with their patients and how they respond to what their patients say. Several core elements of MI technique are represented in the acronym OARS; these core elements are detailed below.

Core techniques of motivational interviewing

Open-ended questions. Therapists should ask their patients open-ended questions, which may roughly be defined as questions that are difficult to answer with one word, like "yes" or "no." Open-ended questions often begin with why ("Why is drinking a concern to you?"), what ("What do you see as the plusses of making changes in your drinking?"), how ("How do you think you might go about making that change?"), or when ("When do you feel is a good time to get started? "). To give an adequate answer to the therapist's open-ended question, the patient must elaborate and describe in some detail relevant thoughts or feelings. The assumption is that, through the process of answering open-ended questions, the patient begins to explore his or her own feelings and thoughts about change toward the end of making decisions about change that are right for him or her. On the other hand, responding to close-ended questions tends not to allow opportunity for such self-exploration about change.

Clinical Pearl
OARS – Core Elements of Motivational Interviewing

O = Open-ended questions	Ask questions that invite detailed answers.
A = Affirmations	Use statements that emphasize client's strengths and efforts.
R = Reflections	Reflect back client statements to clarify and gain additional information.
S = Summaries	Offer summaries to show understanding and to transition to new topics.

Affirmations. "Affirmations" means that the therapist recognizes the patient's strengths, positive values, intentions, successes, and efforts to change. The therapist is specific in "affirming" the patient ("It seems that you've been working hard to keep your alcohol use below 10 drinks this week") rather than global ("What a good job you've done this week").

Reflections. Reflections are a hallmark of MI. The application of this technique in interacting with patients is designed both to demonstrate empathy with the patient and to elicit from him or her as much expression about change as possible. Reflections are a guess about what the patient means and a statement, but not a question. There are several types of reflections, including a simple repetition of what the patient has said ("You feel depressed today"), a paraphrase or a reframe ("So, it seems that you're beginning to think more about how your drinking is worrying you, because it's worrying your husband"), or double-sided ("On the one hand it seems that you enjoy the social ease you feel when you drink, but on the other hand you're beginning to wonder if you can get by socially without drinking"). As noted earlier, reflections are used to gain a greater understanding of the patient's thoughts and feelings regarding some behavior and can be used as well to guide the conversation toward change talk, which is discussed later.

Summaries. Summaries are a critical part of MI and often are underused. They may be defined as a series of reflections that are used strategically during the MI session to assure that the therapist understands what the patient has said, to synthesize important themes running through the conversation with the patient, and to bridge to a new topic in the conversation.

The OARS techniques emphasize actions that therapists initiate to achieve the goals of the MI session, moving the patient toward behavior change. The acronym DARN emphasizes therapist skills in listening for "change talk" (see Clinical Pearl below).

Clinical Pearl
DARN – How to Listen for "Change Talk"

D = Desire	Therapists should be attentive to patient remarks that signal desire to change, some of which are explicit ("I want to stop drinking") and others of which are more subtle or vague ("something about my life has to change").
A = Ability	Therapists also need to be attuned to patients' comments on their perceived ability to make changes ("I've quit smoking already, and reducing my drinking couldn't be any harder than that").
R = Reasons	Therapists attend to patients' stated reasons for change. There are potentially as many different sets of examples as there are patients and such statements often refer to negative health ("I'm worried that drinking is affecting my liver") or social ("I think I've lost some friends over the way I act sometimes when I drink") consequences of heavy alcohol consumption.
N = Need	The last letter of DARN stands for need to change. Need refers to therapists' listening for statements by the patient that signify an urgency of some degree to change. Examples are "I'll only see my kids again if I stop drinking," or "I'm exhausted from waking up with a hangover most mornings."

Why is listening for change talk so important? According to MI methods, change talk is the beginning of the chain to change action. The second step in the chain is the patient's making a commitment to change ("I will reduce my drinking"), which then is presumed to lead to the act of making change itself.

When therapists identify change talk, they of course need to respond to it in a way that is effective, that is, in a way that is likely to help move the patient toward making a commitment to change. MI suggests several ways to respond to change talk effectively. These include reflection ("The costs of heavy drinking seem to be going up"), asking for more information ("Could you tell me some other reasons why change might make sense for you?"), and use of summary (collect and reiterate the themes expressed throughout the patient's change talk). Listening for change talk and using empathic listening are demonstrated in the Clinical Vignette that follows.

We have incorporated several of the principles of MI/ME into the Clinical Vignette below. Notice that the therapist starts with an open-ended question, and then makes use of affirmations, reflections, and a summary (OARS). Most of the therapist's responses are framed in terms of a statement (reflection), rather than as a question. This demonstrates empathy; it shows that the therapist is listening and has heard what the patient has said. Such statements encourage the patient to say more without feeling like they are being interrogated. Also notice that many of the statements that the therapist chooses to follow-up on could be labeled as "change talk." Each of the patient's change statements could be categorized into one of the four DARN categories (desire, ability, reason, need).

Clinical Vignette
Empathic Listening and Listening for Change Talk

Therapist: Last week I showed you how your drinking compares to others', and I'm wondering, now that you've had some time to think about it, how you are feeling about that feedback?

Patient: Well, I guess I never thought that my drinking was any different than anyone else's. All of my friends drink about the same amount I do. But I know that I spend a lot of money on beer.

Therapist: So, you're concerned about the amount of money that you spend.

Patient: Sure. But that's not really the main problem. I'm worried about what kind of a message I might be sending to my kids. I don't want them to think I'm an alcoholic.

Therapist: You're worried that your kids might see you as an alcoholic.

Patient: Well, maybe I am an alcoholic. It seems that I drink a lot more than the average guy, right? But over the past week, I've really tried to pay attention to how much I'm drinking.

Therapist: That's a great start – paying more attention to how much you drink.

Patient: I'm sure that drinking is having some effect on my health.

Therapist: You've mentioned several important things. You're concerned about how much you spend, about what your kids might think, and about whether you might be an alcoholic. And you're also wondering about the effects that drinking might have on your health.

Patient: My kids are the most important thing. I don't want them to follow in my footsteps. I know I can change, and I need to do it for them.

It of course is possible that a patient expresses little, if any, change talk during a MI session. In that case, then the part of MI that is "directive" may come into play to shape the conversation toward more frequent change talk. Some techniques that commonly are used include selective reflection, selective requests for elaboration, or, especially when the patient volunteers little to no change talk, use of exercises to elicit it. One such exercise is the decisional balance, in which the therapist and patient systematically explore the advantages (pros) of not changing a behavior and the disadvantages (cons) of not changing that behavior, as well as the pros and cons of changing. Decisional balance is discussed in greater depth in Chapter 3, and we have provided a decisional balance exercise in the Appendix.

General Summary

In summary, MI consists of several techniques that are designed to elicit patient talk about change (OARS) and that are assumed to cause statements of commitment to change. Commitment then leads to action. These techniques are applied in an interpersonal context of therapist and patient that is patient-centered and that emphasizes the patient's ability to make the changes that he or she desires and take responsibility for doing so. It is important to note in this regard that the style of therapist-patient interaction that MI/ME promotes may be used to advantage in any method of interpersonal psychotherapy. For the reader who is interested in learning more about MI, we have recommended several excellent books under Further Readings (e.g., Center for Substance Abuse Treatment, 1999; Miller & Rollnick, 2002; Rollnick, Mason, & Butler, 1999).

4.2.3   Cognitive Behavioral Approaches

Cognitive-behavioral therapy (CBT) for alcohol and other drug use disorders includes several approaches that differ in aspects such as duration, modality, content, and treatment setting. However, all of these approaches share two essential elements. First, some sort of coping skills training is included in them to address the patient's deficits. Second, CBT approaches are applications of social cognitive theory (Bandura, 1986). It also is worth noting that CBT approaches are called "broad spectrum," because they do not merely focus on the drinking response, but instead address the array of the individual's life functioning. These points will become more apparent as we explore the theoretical foundations of CBT.

Theoretical Foundation

The theoretical foundations for cognitive-behavioral therapy (CBT)

Social cognitive theory (SCT) is the derivative of social learning theory (SLT); Albert Bandura was the chief architect of both theories (1969, 1977, 1986). SLT maintains that human functioning involves interrelated control systems in which behavior is determined by external stimulus events, by internal processing systems and regulatory codes, and by reinforcing response-feedback systems. This fundamental conception of human nature has not changed in the last 40 years.

In current social cognitive theory, there are four primary constructs that are relevant to our understanding of CBT approaches. The first of these is *differential reinforcement*, which refers to the application of consequences for a behavior dependent on stimulus conditions. "Stimulus conditions" broadly define the "setting." Differential reinforcement may involve positive or negative reinforcement, or punishment, or withdrawal of these three events and often occurs directly from the external environment. It also is critical to note that differential consequences for a behavior may be from an external source, be self-administered, or occur vicariously.

The second major construct is *vicarious learning*. This refers to learning through observation of others, or through communication by symbolic means, such as spoken or written language. Vicarious learning assumed a more prominent role, in contrast to learning by direct experience, in the evolution of SLT to social cognitive theory.

The third major construct is *cognitive processes*, which also have become more important in later versions of SLT/SCT compared to earlier ones. Cognitions are viewed as mediating environmental events and behavior. A major piece of information that individuals derive from the environment is consequences for a behavior, and thus *expectancies* (of behavioral outcomes) play a prominent role in regulating behavior. Another concept that is relevant here is self-regulatory functions, which gave rise to the importance of *self-efficacy* in the enactment of behavior.

The final major construct is *reciprocal determinism*, which later became triadic reciprocity or the view that the person, the environment, and behavior are interlocking determinants of each other. The amount of influence that each of these inter-related sets of factors has on each other depends on the setting and the behavior in question. Moreover, the "person" factors refer primarily to cognitive processes.

SCT/SLT Underpinnings of CBT
The CBT approach to substance use and disorders has been most heavily influenced by SLT/SCT, as illustrated by the nine major points in the Clinical Pearl below (adapted from Marlatt & Gordon, 1985, pp. 9–10).

Clinical Pearl
Nine Major Points Underlying Cognitive Behavior Therapy

---

1. Addictive behaviors represent a category of learned maladaptive behaviors. Biological factors may predispose one to addiction, but patterns of use are learned.

2. Addictive behaviors occur on a continuum of use.

3. All points along the continuum are influenced by the same principles of learning.

4. Addictive behaviors are learned habits that can be analyzed like any other habit.

5. The determinants of addictive behavior are situational and environmental factors, beliefs and expectations, and the person's family history and prior learning experiences with the substance or activity. Consequences also control addictive behavior.

Clinical Pearl (continued)

6. Social factors are important in the acquisition and performance of addictive behavior.

7. Addictive behaviors often are emitted under stressful conditions. In that respect, they represent maladaptive coping responses.

8. Addictive behaviors are strongly affected by expectations of achieving desired effects by engaging in the addictive behavior. Self-efficacy (to cope with a situation without substance use) also is a determinant of use.

9. The acquisition of new skills and cognitive strategies in a self-management program can result in change in addictive behavior. The new behaviors come under the control of cognitive processes of awareness and decision-making, giving the individual responsibility for behavior change and its maintenance.

Active Ingredients of CBT

There are several components or "active ingredients" that are unique to CBT and that are thought to be responsible for behavior change. These active ingredients are detailed in the Clinical Pearl below.

Clinical Pearl
Active Ingredients in CBT

Unique active ingredients in CBT:

- Functional analysis of substance use.
- Individualized training in recognizing and coping with craving, managing thoughts about substance use, problem solving, planning for emergencies, recognizing seemingly irrelevant decisions, and refusal skills.
- Examination of the patient's cognitive processes related to substance use.
- Identification and debriefing of past and future high-risk situations.
- Encouragement and review of extra-session implementation of skills.
- Practice of skills within sessions.

Active ingredients that could be part of CBT but are not unique to it:

- Discussing, reviewing, and reformulating the patient's goals of treatment.
- Monitoring other (than primary) substance use and general functioning.
- Developing and maintaining a strong therapeutic relationship.
- Assessing family support and possible inclusion in treatment.

Mechanisms of Action

The essential CBT approach to the treatment of substance use disorders hypothesizes that changes in substance use as a result of treatment occur through changes in coping skills (to moderate or stop substance use) and in self-efficacy to do so. However, despite a number of studies testing these hypotheses, there is little evidence to support them (Morgenstern & Longabaugh, 2000). When we review specialized cases of CBT approaches (e.g., behavioral couples therapy, contingency management and community reinforcement, relapse prevention), we will address support of the presumed mechanisms of action for their efficacy or effectiveness in changing substance use patterns.

Basic CBT Methods

With this conceptual foundation, we are now ready to discuss the specifics of CBT treatment methods. We will begin with what we call "basic CBT," which focuses on a functional analysis of substance use and coping skills training. Basic CBT has been administered in varying formats (group or individual) and for different durations or number of sessions. More recent applications of CBT, not surprisingly, are briefer than their predecessors. For example, the manual version by Carroll (1998) that guides much of this discussion was designed to include 11 one-hour sessions if a significant other session is included. Ad hoc sessions can be included if clinically judged to be necessary. This duration and structure of treatment also show that our description of CBT has moved us into the area of more traditional "specialty" substance abuse treatment. This is in contrast to motivational interviewing and BIs, which in general are one session with one or more brief follow-ups and may be administered in a variety of settings, such as primary care or medical emergency departments. Even motivational enhancement typically lasts two sessions (plus an assessment session) with follow-ups and may be delivered in nonsubstance abuse treatment settings.

Functional analysis. Because CBT follows an idiographic (individualized) approach to the design of treatment and the biopsychosocial model of the substance use disorders, the foundation of CBT treatment is a multidimensional assessment of the individual's substance use and related areas of functioning (see Chapter 3). Within an initial assessment of the individual, the functional analysis (FA) is the keystone and is the uniquely "behavioral" influence on CBT interventions. A FA has been defined in different ways; when applied to alcohol or other drug treatment, it most often refers to the biopsychosocial antecedents (stimuli that precede a behavior) and consequences (shorter-term and longer-term, in reference to the occurrence of the behavior) for a given behavior. In our case, the central behavior is some pattern of alcohol use, typically of the sort that has played a big part in bringing the patient into treatment.

The idea that a FA is essential stems from viewing alcohol use as a voluntary behavior that is under the control of identifiable antecedent stimuli (often called "triggers" in clinical settings) and consequences. Functional analyses are assumed to advance treatment because they provide a blueprint for what antecedents or consequences might be altered to modify the alcohol use pattern. Functional analyses also help to identify alternatives to alcohol use in given antecedent conditions that may be healthier and rewarding ("reinforcing") to the individual, with the intent that the alternative behaviors become more likely to occur in the future. It follows from these ideas that the FA is critical to basic CBT because it provides the information needed for individualized coping skills and problem solving training.

In clinical practice, standardized assessment measures may be used to complete a FA, as discussed in Chapter 3. We have included a worksheet in the Appendix of this volume that can be used for this purpose. However, in the vast majority of cases in clinical settings, functional analyses are completed by individual interview. The following Clinical Pearl (based on Center for Substance Abuse Treatment, 1999) demonstrates this process.

The methods of basic CBT

Conducting a functional analysis of drinking is central to CBT

Clinical Pearl
Conducting a Functional Analysis in a Clinical Context

1. Draw two columns on a sheet of paper, headed "triggers" and "effects." Then say, "I'd like to see how alcohol use has fit into the rest of your life."

2. Identify the patient's antecedents: "Tell me about situations in which you've been most likely to drink or use drugs in the past, or of times when you've tended to drink or use more. These might be times when you were with specific people, in specific places, or at certain times of day, or maybe when you were feeling a particular way." Listen reflectively as the patient responds; write down each antecedent in the triggers column.

3. After the patient seems to have reported all triggers, then ask what he or she liked about drinking or using drugs. This is designed to elicit expectations or perceptions of substance effects, not necessarily actual consequences. Write down each desired consequence in the effects column.

4. Once the patient has finished reporting antecedents and consequences, point out how a trigger can lead to a certain effect. Ask the patient to identify "pairs" of triggers and effects from the two columns just created.

Coping skills training is a central theme in CBT

Coping skills training. Coping skills training methods draw primarily from the principles of learning mentioned earlier: operant conditioning, vicarious conditioning, and classical conditioning. Over the years that CBT has been implemented in the treatment of the substance use disorders, coping skills training has been done in many ways. A manual that Monti, Abrams, Kadden, and Cooney published in 1989 that focused on the treatment of alcohol dependence (a second edition of this manual has since been published; Monti, Kadden, Rohsenow, Cooney & Abrams, 2002) was the basis of the CBT intervention that was tested as part of Project MATCH in the 1990s. This manual was influential in providing an empirically supported standard for the application of coping skills training in the treatment of alcohol dependence. Carroll's (1998) manual for the application of a CBT approach in the treatment of cocaine addiction follows in this same line and is the basis for the coping skills training description here.

In CBT, learning is the main theme that runs throughout treatment. In this regard, the therapist makes clear to the patient that alcohol and other drug use behaviors are learned and, as such, their modification is a matter of systematically going about unlearning these behaviors. Patients are receptive and can grasp this idea, in that they can see that if they were able to learn a complex set of behaviors that are called "alcohol use" or "alcohol abuse," then it also is possible to unlearn them and to learn new alternative behaviors. The "strategies" for unlearning old behaviors and learning alternatives (i.e., coping skills training) follow the principles of learning mentioned earlier.

Modeling. The patient participates in role-plays with the therapist to acquire new (coping) behaviors in a given situation or to strengthen behaviors that are unfamiliar or infrequently enacted. The patient observes the therapist perform the newer behaviors and then practices them during the therapy session.

Operant conditioning. The functional analysis is the basis of learning more effective coping behaviors in "high-risk" situations, or as a guide to developing alternative (to alcohol use) thoughts or behavior in such situations that are reinforcing (typically rewarding) to the individual. A detailed analysis of the shorter- and longer-term consequences of use, as delineated in the functional analysis, also can help to sustain motivation to change abusive drinking.

Classical conditioning. Principles of classical conditioning are added to our earlier discussion of learning principles and are especially important in instances where craving (to use alcohol) may be an important antecedent of actual use. In this regard, when an individual enters a situation highly associated with alcohol use, the stimuli (people, location, drug paraphernalia) defining the setting may elicit craving to use alcohol and in turn cause actual use. This occurs through a process of classical conditioning: Through repeated pairings of formerly neutral (regarding alcohol use) stimuli (such as a favorite brand of hard liquor or some physical location like a specific room of a house) with actual alcohol use and its immediate effects, the formerly neutral stimuli acquire alcohol craving-eliciting properties. The therapist, through use of the functional analysis, helps the patient to identify such classically conditioned stimuli in the patient's environment and to either avoid them or to cope with them more effectively when confronted with them by not drinking. Also by principles of classical conditioning, if the patient is exposed to high-risk situations repeatedly without drinking, the power of the stimuli in that setting to elicit craving or urges to drink will be reduced significantly or eliminated.

Therapists need to apply several major principles in implementing coping skills training. First, it is important to teach the patient *generalizable skills*. In this regard, CBT is a briefer therapy, and there is insufficient time to teach patients a new skill for every high-risk situation identified in a functional analysis to achieve treatment goals, for example. Therefore, basic skills are taught in CBT, with an emphasis in the beginning of CBT on skills needed for the patient to control his or her alcohol use in the natural environment. It also is emphasized that the skills taught, say, to cope with craving, may be applied to other high-risk situations, such as those defined by negative emotions as triggers of alcohol use.

Therapists *teach basic skills first*. As we said earlier, skills taught to help a patient initiate and maintain control over alcohol use, and the motivation to sustain such control, are taught first. Later training, such as general problem solving skills, builds upon earlier training. Another important principle is to *tailor training to the patient's needs*. Therapists use the functional analysis to match the content, timing, duration, and format (e.g., complexity of language used) of skills training to the patient's needs. For example, the content of skill training that is taught and practiced is selected according to what is most relevant to the patient's life at that time. Besides having the likely effect of the patient's increased engagement in treatment, it also likely will have the benefit of winning the patient's perception that the therapist has connected to and recognizes what is important to the patient. Related to this latter point, it also is important that therapists frequently check with patients that the therapist's skill-training efforts are relevant to the patient and are meeting the patient's needs. A final point in this regard is that therapists may use current content as the basis of role-plays ("Were there any situations this past week in which you were tempted to drink and had trouble avoiding use, or situations in which you did drink even though you didn't want to?"). Finally, the functional analysis, again, may be the reference for deriving skills training content from situations in which the patient has consumed alcohol heavily in the past.

Therapists also *use repetition*. Patients may have difficulty learning the new behaviors that the therapist is trying to teach during a session for a number of possible reasons, such as preoccupation with current life circumstances, the cognitive consequences of chronic heavy alcohol use, or because alcohol use and associated behaviors are highly ingrained habits. Accordingly, repetition of key concepts is a part of CBT. Finally, it is important that patients *practice mastering skills*. Skills that the patient are taught are practiced both within and outside of the therapy session. Related to this point is a hallmark feature of CBT, "homework" assignments, in which a patient is given instructions to complete specific behavioral tasks in the natural environment between therapy sessions. Homework completion early in treatment has been associated with treatment retention (Gonzalez, Schmitz, & DeLaune, 2006), and homework compliance is a consistent predictor of improved psychotherapy outcomes (Kazantzis, Deane, & Ronan, 2000). It is notable that, as assigning homework has been a feature of behavior therapies since their inception, so has been a difficulty in patient compliance with completing the assignments. Therefore, it is essential that the therapist follow-up and monitor the patient's completion of homework both as a key to mastering the skills that have been assessed as needed for change and to have an ongoing evaluation of the patient's engagement in treatment. Kazantzis and colleagues have offered a number of useful guidelines for maximizing the clinical utility of homework assignments (see Kazantzis, Deane, & Ronan, 2004; Kazantzis, Deane, Ronan, & L'Abate, 2005).

With these general principles in mind, the content of skills emphasized in CBT may include coping with urges, alcohol or other drug use refusal skills/assertiveness training, the development of a general coping plan, and problem solving methods. Note, again, that what skills are emphasized and how much time is spent teaching them are determined primarily by the patient's needs as delineated in the functional analysis and by current life events.

Coping with urges involves first discussing with the patient what urges and craving are and that they may persist for weeks or months after use of alcohol has stopped. The therapist then uses a functional analysis approach to identify antecedents for craving reactions. Based on this analysis, skills are taught and practiced to help the individual handle cravings without use. Techniques that might be taught to the patient include, first and most basically, avoiding the settings that tend to elicit cravings. However, it is inevitable that situations that elicit craving will be encountered by some patients, and techniques that have been developed to help them deal with such situations include distraction, talking with trusted and supportive friends about the cravings, going with the cravings (that is, "staying" with them as they rise, peak, and decline in intensity) without fighting or yielding to them, recalling the negative consequences of drinking, and using "positive self-talk" to counteract automatic thoughts that often accompany cravings and carry the message that the patient "must" drink. We have included a worksheet in the Appendix (High-Risk for Drinking Situations – Identification and Coping Strategies) that can be used to help patients identify their high-risk situations and to plan for the coping strategies that can be used in each situation.

Refusal skills/assertiveness training involves teaching the patient general assertiveness skills, with particular attention to applying them to cope with social pressure in the patient's environment to drink. These skills may be important for many patients because, through their entrenchment in a lifestyle that centers on alcohol use, they may have few social contacts who are not active alcohol or other drug users.

Development of a general coping plan addresses the fact that life often deals us unexpected events, both positive and negative, that we deal with one way or another. The key here is that, for individuals with an alcohol use disorder, such unexpected events may become potent triggers to drink if abstinence is desired or to drink heavily if moderation is the goal. Developing a general coping plan is designed to help the patient anticipate possible events that could occur in the next several months that potentially could be triggers to drink or to drink heavily and to plan ways to cope with these events should they occur without resorting to undesired alcohol or other drug use.

Problem solving methods are the capstone of coping skills training in a sense. In this regard, the patient is taught the basic steps in problem solving that have been presented in the behavioral literature for decades. By learning and mastering these steps, patients become equipped to handle situations that require action in general, regardless of whether they directly are or were connected to alcohol use. In that way, patients' functioning in multiple areas may be improved.

4.3   Extensions of Basic CBT

Basic CBT is primarily an individual-oriented approach. This means that the focus of treatment, whether it is delivered in an individual or group format, or if it includes one or more "couples" sessions, is on the individual identified as having the alcohol problem. That individual is viewed as the agent of change. Therefore, even if the antecedents and consequences of alcohol consumption are identified to be social-interpersonal and involve friends or family members, the individual is the vehicle through which changes in those social factors are made. For example, this goal may be achieved by the individual's initiating change in his or her social network to one that reinforces abstinence from alcohol or drugs or a reduction in their use. Another example is that the individual is guided in initiating changes in the environment, as in systematically avoiding high-risk situations that may or may not involve other people.

4.3.1   Behavioral Couples Therapy

Behavioral couples therapy (BCT) follows CBT principles but changes the level of focus from the individual to the dyadic relationship. Most often, BCT has been studied when the relationship includes the person with the alcohol problem and his or her spouse, but it also has been used with other close relationships, such as cohabiting committed partners who are not married, the identified alcohol abuser's mother or father, his or her sibling or other fam-

The focus of behavioral couples therapy is on the dyadic relationship

ily member, or close friend. Typically, the alcohol abuser and the significant other have been living together for at least one year. In addition, BCT has been evaluated when the alcohol abuser's "significant other" who is accompanying him or her in treatment does not have an alcohol or drug problem, but more recent work has included relationships in which both members of the relationship have an alcohol or drug problem.

BCT's premise is that family members and other individuals close to the alcohol abuser can have a large influence on his or her alcohol or other drug use by reinforcing abstinence or moderation. In addition, BCT assumes that alcohol abusers who are from happier homes or who are happily engaged in close social networks that reinforce nonproblem substance use (abstinence or moderation, depending on treatment goals) are at a lower risk for relapse. (We will have more to say about relapse and its prevention later; suffice it to say for now that relapse may be defined as a return to levels of problem alcohol or drug use after a period of nonproblem use (abstinence or moderation) that the patient voluntarily initiated and hoped to sustain.) BCT has enjoyed a considerable history of empirical demonstrations of its efficacy when used to treat primary alcohol or other substance use disorders, and there are several excellent practically oriented sources on the topic. This summary draws primarily from the work of O'Farrell and Fals-Stewart (2000, 2002, 2003). Our discussion assumes that the alcohol abuser and his or her spouse are in treatment, as that situation allows a full exposition of techniques that constitute BCT.

Mechanisms of Action
As with basic CBT, the mechanisms of action of BCT include changes in self-efficacy and an improvement in coping skills, especially an improvement in communication skills between partners in a significant relationship. However, for BCT, another mechanism of change is improvement in the couple's relationship (defined in several different ways, such as satisfaction, or support for abstinence from alcohol or moderation of consumption).

BCT Components
BCT may be administered in 15–20 one-hour outpatient sessions over a period of about 5–6 months. It has two main categories of components, which are designed to achieve control over the alcohol abuser's alcohol consumption and to improve the relationship between the couple, or among other family members and close friends as applicable, respectively. We describe each briefly here.

Sobriety contracts are often used in BCT

Controlling alcohol use: Sobriety contract. The purpose of the sobriety contract is to have a structured way for the alcohol abuser's partner to build support for and reinforce abstinence or moderation, according to the designated alcohol use outcome goal. The contract includes several parts. First, if abstinence is the goal, and if the alcohol abuser is willing and is cleared medically, he or she agrees to take medication such as disulfiram, naltrexone, or acamprosate as prescribed as an aid to achieving and maintaining sobriety. Attendance at mutual self-help group meetings may also be part of the contract. Furthermore, the contract includes the alcohol abuser's daily expression of his or her intent to sustain abstinence or moderation in use. The spouse, in turn, agrees to reinforce these behaviors every day. The contract also includes an agreement by the alcohol abuser's spouse not to bring up fears of future drinking or anger about past drinking outside of the therapy session. The occurrence of all of these "terms" of the contract as relevant are marked on a calendar that the therapist provides. The couple brings the completed calendar to therapy sessions, and the therapist reviews it at the beginning of each one. The therapist rewards successful performance but also provides feedback to troubleshoot any difficulties that the couple experiences in implementing the contract.

Of course, initial methods at getting the patient's drinking under control are not always successful. In such cases, BCT has included the use of several different methods. The first is one that Barbara McCrady and her colleagues (1986) described that was designed to reduce the frequency of behaviors among family members that may trigger an individual's abusive drinking or inadvertently encourage ("enable") it. Collectively, these interventions are called "alcohol-focused spouse involvement" (AFSI) and involve teaching the alcohol abuser's spouse how to reinforce a reduction in drinking and to decrease the frequency of behaviors that may inadvertently encourage alcohol use by shielding the alcohol abuser from the negative consequences of his or her drinking. Essentially, AFSI is based on the results of a functional analysis of the alcohol abuser's use that focuses on the spouse and other family members as "antecedent stimuli" (triggers) of alcohol use or as reinforcers of use.

A second aspect of BCT that is used if there is difficulty in getting the alcohol use under control is that the patient is asked to maintain a daily record of urges to drink or use drugs (following the FA format), which is reviewed at the beginning of each BCT session. This daily record is based on the premise that it is important to address abusive substance use early before it becomes a severe problem with its concomitant consequences and threat to the couple's commitment to treatment.

However, if abusive drinking (or other drug use) does occur, BCT attempts to present the "relapse" as a learning experience, and not a failure experience. This approach is in line with the methods of relapse prevention, which we will discuss later. The therapist also works to temper any negative affect that is associated with the occurrence of alcohol use and to help the couple get the alcohol abuser to control his or her drinking again. In some cases, the resumption of sobriety may involve detoxification or some other major adjustment in the treatment plan.

If alcohol or other drug use continues at abusive levels, then the functional analysis may be used to identify its determinants. The couple's relationship may or may not be identified as an important factor in this regard. If the determinants are outside of the relationship (say, work or other social factors), then individual sessions with the alcohol abuser that focus on those factors may be added to the intervention. However, the relationship may be a cause of recurrent use of alcohol or other drugs. For example, communication or sex may seem to be improved when the alcohol abuser is intoxicated. In such cases, the therapist works with the couple to help them attain the same positive outcomes without the use of alcohol or other drugs. In other cases, the alcohol use may actually be adaptive to the relationship in that it seems to help resolve some conflicts. In that context, the couple is taught communication skills that may help them to achieve the same ends in a way that has healthier longer-term consequences. This approach is reflected in the second part of BCT, which focuses on improving the couple's relationship.

Improving the couple's relationship: Exercises and homework assignments. BCT includes the assignment of various exercises or tasks that are learned in the therapy session but are designed to be practiced extensively outside of sessions as "homework," much as described in our discussion of coping skills training and basic CBT. These tasks and exercises have the goals of enhancing the degree of reinforcement that both partners receive from their relationship, increasing the number of shared activities that partners engage in that do not involve alcohol use, and improving constructive communication skills. Together they constitute ways to improve the marital relationship once the alcohol use is under control. Including these components in BCT is based on the premise that, if the alcohol abuser is in a relationship that is reinforcing (i.e., a source of positive feelings), includes ample shared activities that do not involve drinking, and that is able to address problems constructively by use of good communication skills, then he or she is more likely to sustain sobriety or moderation of alcohol use. The specific exercises or tasks are as follows.

Increasing the frequency of caring behaviors. The therapist defines caring behaviors to the couple as behaviors showing that one cares for another person. In BCT, the goal is to increase the frequency of the initiation of and the acknowledgement of the occurrence of such behaviors by each partner for the other. The assumption is that such an increase in caring behaviors will enhance the positive feelings that emanate from being in the relationship and therefore its value to each partner. Two exercises are included toward the end of increasing the frequency of caring behaviors. The first is called *catch your spouse (partner) doing something nice.* The therapist asks each partner to write down one caring behavior each day that he or she notices was initiated by the other and to write it down on a sheet of paper that the therapist provides. The list of caring behaviors is brought to the next therapy session and is read aloud. The therapist then models the communication skill of acknowledging the caring behavior, and both partners practice that skill in the therapy session. The homework assignment for each partner is to notice at least one caring behavior from the other partner each day and to take 5–10 minutes acknowledging its occurrence. The planning of *caring days* is the second part of implementing the goal of increasing the frequency of caring behaviors in the relationship. In this exercise the assignment is for each partner to show how much he or she cares for the other partner by planning and carrying out a "caring day" by doing special acts or engaging in special activities. Both "catch your partner" and "caring days" tend to result in the sought-after increase in positive actions by each partner toward the other, improved communication (initiated by acknowledging caring acts), and an increase in positive feelings about the relationship. Importantly, initiating these positive behaviors often engenders positive feelings, which seem essential to returning the relationship to a stronger and healthier state. On the other hand, given the state of many relationships affected by alcohol abuse, if partners waited for positive feelings before initiating reinforcing behaviors, the relationship might not stand the time that that could take to happen.

Planning and engaging in shared recreational activities. The partners agree to plan and engage in recreational activities that they can do together (or that include other family members or adults) that do not involve alcohol use. Initiating such activities is important because of their association with improved treatment outcomes. The therapist might help the partners begin this assignment by simply listing with them possible activities that could be engaged in. It also might be useful to model planning an actual activity, so that any logistical or other obstacles might be avoided or managed without difficulty.

Teaching improved communication skills. We already have referred to the use of communication skills in discussing several facets of BCT. In BCT, the therapist introduces and models techniques of constructive communication that are practiced and mastered by the couple outside of therapy sessions. These skills focus on conflict resolution, which is a critical factor in couples involving an alcohol abusing partner. Communication skills training proceeds in a way similar to that described for coping skills training and basic CBT.

Controlling alcohol use: Relapse prevention. The final BCT component is relapse prevention. In this component, the couple completes a "continuing recovery plan" at the end of each weekly BCT session. The plan is reviewed quarterly during a two-year follow-up period that is part of BCT. The continuing recovery plan has several parts. First, the partners decide which of the behaviors initiated as part of BCT (e.g., sobriety contract) that they wish to continue. Second, the couple is encouraged to anticipate what high-risk situations may be encountered and to devise nonalcohol or other drug-using ways to cope with them (i.e., what effective coping skills will be used in the high-risk situations). Third, the couple anticipates and practices how it will handle a relapse to abusive drinking should it happen. Related to this point, it is essential that the therapist emphasize that intervention occur as early as possible should a relapse occur.

4.3.2 Contingency Management and Community Reinforcement

If BCT changes the level of focus from the individual to the interpersonal dyad and family system, community reinforcement (CR) shifts the focus another level "up" to that of the larger social system. Here the social "system" in question may of course include the patient's spouse, for example, but may also extend further to larger groups of different kinds and even, conceptually, societal factors such as practices and norms regarding alcohol use. The essential interest is the system's reinforcement or nonreinforcement of abusive alcohol or other drug use.

The community reinforcement approach incorporates the drinker's larger social system

CR also is notable among the CBT approaches because of its greater reliance on behavioral (meaning based on principles and theories of learning new information) factors rather than cognitive variables, and a good link to that slant is contingency management (CM) and the use of vouchers. As we will see, both CM and CR are based in principles of operant conditioning. We will begin with a brief description of contingency management and the use of vouchers, as it is the most "purely operant" of the CBT procedures and thus provides a good transition to our description of CR. You also will recognize parts of CM and CR in our earlier descriptions of basic CBT and BCT.

Contingency Management

The basis and method of CM lie in principles of reinforcement and punishment, and its methods are straightforward: Reinforce behavior that is consistent with the attainment of treatment goals and withhold reinforcement for off-goal behavior. By virtue of its contents, CM is primarily an individual-based approach that does not require a large number of sessions to administer. However, it is common that CM methods are used as part of broader treatment programs or procedures, and in those contexts the amount of time or emphasis placed on CM would vary according to the additional treatment in question.

The core of contingency management is the reinforcement of abstinence

The core of CM is to reinforce abstinence (or moderation, as the case may be) from alcohol use and to withhold reinforcement for alcohol use or abuse. The idea is to stabilize control over drinking to allow other lifestyle changes to develop. (This is reminiscent of BCT and the sobriety contract.) "Reinforcement" may take many forms, but clinically vouchers have been used effectively. Vouchers are promissory notes that the therapist administers to the patient for the patient's achieving specified substance use goals and may be exchanged for a diverse array of items such as clothing, tickets to a movie, gift certificates from a book store, or electronic goods. Probably the main restrictions on the form that a voucher takes are that it be consistent with treatment goals, is subject to therapist approval, and, if relevant, is purchased by program staff. Cash would not be used as an incentive for sobriety, because it can readily be exchanged for alcohol or other drugs. In addition, patients earn "points" toward their reinforcers, with increasing point payments made as length of time on goal increases. On the other hand, if the patient is off-goal, then points are withheld, but previously earned points are not lost. When the patient has earned the stipulated number of points, then he or she is entitled to receive the reinforcer chosen.

In CM, behavior–consequences relationships often are implemented clinically by use of written, well-specified contracts between the patient and therapist. CM may be used as a stand-alone intervention or, as noted earlier, combined with another behavioral or pharmacological treatment method(s). For example, CM has been found to enhance the efficacy of CR in treating cocaine abusers.

Clinical Pearl
Four Administration "Principles" for Current Contingency Management Methods

---

1. Include regular biomarker testing (e.g., breath testing for alcohol) during treatment as an objective reference of determining if the patient's substance use is "on-goal."

2. If abstinence (or moderation) is ascertained, the therapist should provide previously agreed upon reinforcers.

3. If substance use is off-goal, the therapist should withhold reinforcers.

4. The therapist should help the patient develop alternative, reinforcing behaviors to alcohol or other drug use in specified situations that together eventually lead to a nonsubstance abusing lifestyle. (This idea has been integral to community reinforcement methods since their initial publication in 1973.)

Based on Higgins & Petry (1999).

With this brief description of CM, we now turn to a description of CR, which also is heavily based in principles of operant conditioning but always has considered the patient's larger social environment as a source of reinforcement or nonreinforcement/punishment of abusive alcohol or other drug use. Note that the fourth "principle" structuring current administration of CM methods essentially addresses substance abuse at this same larger environment level.

Contingency Management Mechanisms of Action

CM methods view a change to reinforcement for a sober lifestyle rather than for a substance abusing lifestyle, and a change to withholding reinforcement for substance abuse, as the primary mechanisms of change in substance use and related behaviors.

Community Reinforcement

We have already made several references to community reinforcement (CR) methods in the preceding paragraphs. This approach has not changed in major ways since it was first published in the early 1970s. As we will see, it consists of several different components that can be used as needed to help the patient reach his or her treatment goals. In other words, it still is accurate to say that a patient experienced CR treatment even if all of the components that we describe later have not been administered. On the other hand, the evidence is not clear regarding what are the "necessary and sufficient" CR components for this method to be effective with a given patient or patient profile. Along these lines, we present here a description of the full complement of CR components, with the understanding that the approach has empirical support if all are available for use as needed with a given patient.

CR essentially is an individual approach, although as we will see it may include couples sessions. In addition, CR has been administered for durations that have varied widely, but more recent, manual-based versions generally are designed to last about 12 one-hour weekly outpatient sessions as a base.

Community Reinforcement Mechanisms of Action

As with CM, CR methods hypothesize that changes in contingencies of reinforcement for nonuse or moderate alcohol use and withholding of reinforcement for abusive use of alcohol underlie CR treatment effects. In CR, the source of reinforcement contingencies focuses on the individual's social system.

Community Reinforcement Components

We describe here the major CR components that have been applied in empirically supported trials of the approach. Our description is based on several excellent CR summaries, most notably that provided by Meyers, Villanueva, and Smith (2005).

CR functional analysis. As with other CBT approaches, the functional analysis of the individual's alcohol or other drug use is the foundation of the CR approach. It is safe to say that the conduct of a functional analysis is not an "optional" CR component. As with the use of the functional analysis in other CBT approaches, its purpose is to specify the antecedents and consequences

Major components of community reinforcement

of well-defined alcohol use. It is critical in CR to identify the positive consequences for alcohol use that the individual experiences, as they are key to identifying the maintaining conditions that might be altered through treatment, as well as identifying alternative, healthy ("sober") behaviors that might achieve the same degree of reward for the individual.

Sobriety sampling. Sobriety sampling may be used if the patient is reluctant to commit to a goal of abstinence "for eternity," even if his or her problem with alcohol is severe. Sobriety sampling is a way to work toward total abstinence by negotiating with the patient a trial abstinence period, for purposes of experiencing life without alcohol (or other nonprescribed drug) use and, concurrently, building the skills and changes in the social environment that may be needed to help the person achieve a rewarding, sober lifestyle. At the end of the "sobriety sampling period," the patient and therapist renegotiate the drinking outcome goal, with the hope that the trial experience has helped to persuade the patient that life without alcohol or other drugs can be as or more rewarding as life with them.

CR treatment plan. This is another of the essential components of CR as it is with other approaches, as it essentially constitutes formal treatment planning and specification. CR uses two forms to aid in the development of the treatment plan. The first is called the "Happiness Scale," which lists 10 areas of functioning (e.g., job, marriage/family, emotional life) and the patient's degree of satisfaction with them. The data from this exercise provide information for the patient and therapist about what areas that treatment should focus on. When focus areas have been identified, the patient and therapist complete the Goals of Counseling Form. This form lists the same 10 areas probed on the Happiness Scale, and asks for specific goal(s) in each area (if any), ways that they will be achieved (treatment "objectives" in the usual treatment planning language), and a proposed time period for the achievement of each goal. Good goal setting methods are applied, so that goals are written to be specific, obtainable, and progress toward their achievement measurable. The Happiness Scale and the Goals of Counseling Form, as well as completed examples of each, can be found in Meyers & Smith (1995), which is cited under Further Readings.

Behavioral skills training. If the initial functional analysis and treatment planning reveal behavioral skills deficits critical to building a sober lifestyle (or if such deficits are revealed at any other time during treatment), then CR incorporates behavioral skills training. Such training is similar in concept and practice to that described for the other CBT approaches. Behavioral skills training in CR focuses on three areas: general problem solving skills, as we described for basic CBT; communication skills, as we described both in basic CBT and BCT; and drink/drug refusal, which we described earlier in basic CBT.

Job skills. This component is unique to CR among the CBT approaches, in that it is systematically incorporated as part of the treatment itself, instead of, say, accomplished by referral to an outside treatment agent or provider. CR attempts to help patients get jobs if that is needed, because it is reasoned that, at least in Western societies, an individual's job is a critical part of his or her "community." In the original version of CR, part of the treatment was to establish a "job club," which centered all activity on finding a job. Current versions of CR include the use of a "job club manual." Moreover, CR helps individuals determine the degree of satisfaction they are getting from their job if in fact they are employed, and behavioral skills training as cited earlier may be used as needed to help individuals maintain the jobs that they already have, if that is desired.

Social/recreational counseling. This is another component of CR that is unique to CBT approaches in its systematic incorporation as part of the treatment approach. Social/recreational counseling was included in the original CR version for the very important reason that many substance abusers who present for treatment do not have a social network that is alcohol or drug free or even that reinforces abstinence or moderation, and may not have had one for many years. Therefore, consistent with the premise of CR, if needed, patients are helped to develop a social network that encourages a sober and ultimately rewarding lifestyle. Many of the studies of CR actually included a "social club" to facilitate this end. This was a place where sober individuals could meet, primarily on weekends, to socialize. If done effectively, the social club provided a safe place for the individual to practice any social skills learned as part of treatment to help advance a sober lifestyle. The social club also helped to teach the individual initially that social life without alcohol or other drugs could be rewarding.

Relapse prevention. Similar to BCT, this component of CR is an essential part and begins with completion of the initial functional analysis. The functional analysis helps to identify high-risk situations for the individual that then may be anticipated and "practiced for" effectively coping (i.e., in healthy, nonsubstance using ways) with them. As might be surmised, several of the CR components that we have described already (e.g., skills training, social/recreational counseling) contribute to the relapse prevention plan in an ongoing manner during the course of CR treatment.

Relationship counseling. This component follows the premise, structure, and format of couples sessions in BCT. As a critical part of the social community for some patients, marital or other intimate relationships are thought to be highly effective agents of change in the patient's alcohol use if they encourage sobriety (or moderation) and are a source of reinforcement (happiness) to the patient. The content of couples sessions, if included, is structured by use of the "Relationship Happiness Form" (the original form is called the "Marriage Happiness Scale"), a counterpart to the Happiness Scale that was described under treatment planning. Similarly, the "Perfect Relationship Form" (also called the "Perfect Marriage Form") is modeled after the Goals of Counseling Form that was described under treatment planning and helps to identify goals and objectives for achieving a happier, more satisfying, and sober relationship. Finally, CR couples sessions can include activities such as "Daily Reminder to be Nice" to jump-start the occurrence of daily reinforcing behaviors from one partner to the other. The Marriage Happiness Scale, the Perfect Marriage Form, and the Daily Reminder to be Nice (with completed examples) can be found in Meyers and Smith (1995).

Concluding Comment about Community Reinforcement
As should be apparent from even our brief description of CR, it can be a complex and intensive treatment method to deliver, depending on the patient's needs. Nevertheless, years of efficacy trials have identified CR as an empiri-

cally supported alcohol treatment. The problem from the time that the first CR efficacy studies were published, however, is that CR, at least in the United States, has been less than popular in clinical practice. As Meyers et al. (2005) noted, there are several plausible reasons for this science-practitioner gap, including the perception that considerable resources are required, including therapist energy, to implement CR, infrequent or inaccessible opportunities for training in CR, and an "individualistic" (as opposed to a social systems) bias among many alcohol/drug treatment providers in the United States. Overall, it would seem important for practitioners to consider these barriers more closely, assess the degree of impediment that they pose, and to remove them if possible, as CR probably has stronger empirical support than any of the other CBT approaches that we have described. In fact, as you probably have noticed, other CBT approaches have incorporated parts of CR, which preceded them.

4.3.3   Relapse Prevention

Relapse generally refers to a resumption of substance use following a period of abstinence

The term "relapse" has been defined in many ways in the literature, from resumption of any alcohol or other drug use at all following a period of committed abstinence, to the return to pretreatment, or "prevoluntary change," levels of alcohol or other drug use and related problems. There also are prominent clinical researchers who believe that the use of the term relapse itself is steeped in the biomedical model of addiction and therefore is outmoded and possibly counterproductive. Regardless of the perspective that is taken on how relapse is defined and the utility of continued use of the term in advancing drug and alcohol treatment, relapse is a clinical phenomenon that clinicians and their patients take seriously. Accordingly, there has been a considerable amount of clinical research and practice devoted to the problem of relapse and the substance use disorders, especially since about 1980.

As you may have noted, we have used the term "relapse" frequently in this book in describing different empirically supported treatment methods. In our view, *relapse refers to the return to prechange levels of alcohol or other drug use.* Change may refer to assisted change (whether by formal treatment or other methods such as mutual self-help groups) or simply one's own self-driven behavioral changes. Essentially, use of the word relapse means that the individual has gone off the path of his or her planned course of change. The problems in definition that have been discussed so extensively in the literature have been concerned primarily with what degree of going "off course" defines a relapse, and how many aspects of substance use should be considered in determining whether a relapse has occurred: quantity of drug or alcohol use, frequency of use, duration of use, and/or negative consequences associated with use? In the United States, probably the *most common definition of relapse* that is used in specialty treatment contexts is *any return at all to alcohol or other drug use.* More broadly, we may think of relapse in terms of the patient's substance use outcome goal(s) and the degree of variation from reaching them that an individual is experiencing.

With these brief introductory comments on the definition of relapse, it is clear that all treatment interventions essentially are designed to be methods of change initiation and then maintenance of that change over time. In that sense, all treatment methods may qualify as "relapse prevention" methods. However, in the alcohol and drug treatment area, relapse prevention has a specific meaning, which is methods that have been derived from a CBT model of relapse initially articulated by Alan Marlatt and colleagues in the late 1970s and continually elaborated and expanded upon by them and others since that time. The CBT model of relapse gained wide influence with the publication of Marlatt and Gordon's (1985) book on relapse prevention that fully articulated the CBT model of relapse. The second edition of this book was published in 2005 by Marlatt and Donovan. The CBT approach to relapse prevention (RP) is the set of methods that has empirical support and that is described here.

We actually do not need to provide a separate full description of RP, because it is taken from the general CBT model and methods that we have described in some detail. In addition, we already have described much of what RP involves, because it is part of CBT methods that we discussed already in our description of basic CBT, BCT, and CR. Furthermore, RP always was intended to be an "adjunct" intervention, as it was designed to be administered as part of or integrated with a full intervention program. As a result, the clinical research that constitutes the empirical support for RP has evaluated it in such a context. Nevertheless, it still is useful to describe the components of what would formally be recognized as RP among clinicians and clinical researchers. Our description is based on excellent summaries by Marlatt and Witkiewitz (2005) and by Witkiewitz, Marlatt, and Walker (2005).

Relapse Prevention Goals and Components

RP (Marlatt & Donovan, 2005; Marlatt & Gordon, 1985) has two primary goals. The first of these goals is to prevent a "lapse" (a term used to denote *an "initial" or minor deviation from the path of abstinence* or moderation of substance use, depending on the behavior change goal). The second goal is to successfully manage a lapse if it occurs, so as to prevent it from becoming a full relapse. As you might guess from our earlier descriptions of CBT-based methods, RP may be administered as an individual, couples, or group intervention.

Relapse prevention has two goals: preventing a "lapse" to drinking, and managing any lapses that may occur

RP is designed to achieve its aims by first identifying the individual's "high-risk" (for off-goal substance use) situations by use of a functional analysis, and then to use behavioral and cognitive methods of coping with these situations to avert a relapse. When the high-risk situations have been identified (note, however, as we said in our earlier discussions, the functional analysis never should be considered "closed," as relevant new information may become available at any time), the therapist works with the patient to specify coping skills, cognitive factors such as self-efficacy, and lifestyle patterns that may increase the likelihood that the patient copes effectively when he or she encounters high-risk situations.

Behavioral and cognitive interventions also may be used as needed to prevent relapse, and they essentially follow from the original CBT model of relapse that Marlatt created. First, RP has an educational component, in which individuals are challenged about their beliefs about alcohol's beneficial coping effects, which may be based more in myth than in fact. In addition, individuals are instructed about ways of thinking that may be nonproductive or that may help to trigger a lapse or relapse, and are informed about cognitive restructuring of maladaptive thoughts or misperceptions. Furthermore, individuals

Anticipating the "abstinence violation effect"

are taught about the "abstinence violation effect" (AVE), which is a part of Marlatt's original model of relapse and pertains to the negative emotion that may accompany a lapse, combined with expectancies that alcohol or other drugs may help alleviate the resulting aversive state compared to nonsubstance use coping methods that the individual may be aware of or may not feel self-efficacious about using in a particular situation. The danger of the AVE is that, left unchecked, it increases the likelihood that a lapse will become a relapse. Part of the education about the AVE is to inform patients that a lapse is a "normal" part of the course of behavior change that can be managed effectively to place the individual quickly back on the course toward achievement of sustained change in patterns of alcohol use.

RP extends beyond ways of managing high-risk situations to helping the individual build a lifestyle that encourages balance between obligations that may be stressful, such as work and pleasurable activities that do not involve harmful use of alcohol or other drugs. In this way, RP is very much coordinated with the general aims of CBT methods such as BCT and CR. Toward the end of building a more balanced lifestyle, which ultimately works to reduce or eventually eliminate the occurrence of "high-risk" situations, the individual may be taught different behavioral techniques, such as deep muscle relaxation or meditation. The final product of this set of RP activities is that the individual develops a relapse "road map" that identifies high-risk situations, cognitive and behavioral response options in each one, and an analysis of the pros and cons of responding in different ways to a given situation. Again, the "relapse prevention" plans that we cited as part of BCT and CR, for example, are analogous to the idea of a relapse road map. With a detailed road map in hand, presumably the individual is equipped to travel the path to sustained change in patterns of alcohol or other drug use, if that is what is desired. The following Clinical Pearl provides some guidelines for what to do if a relapse occurs. The Pearl is replicated in the Appendix, for use as a patient handout.

Clinical Pearl
What To Do if a Relapse Occurs

1. Use the relapse as a learning experience.

2. See the relapse as a specific, unique event.

3. Examine the relapse openly in order to reduce the amount of guilt and/or shame you may feel (those thoughts can lead to a feeling of hopelessness and continued drinking).

4. Analyze the triggers for the relapse.

5. Examine what the expectations about drinking were at the time (what did you anticipate drinking would accomplish in that situation?).

6. Plan for dealing with the aftermath/consequences of the relapse.

7. Tell yourself that control is only a moment away.

8. Renew your commitment to abstinence (or drinking reduction, if appropriate).

9. Make immediate plans for recovery – don't hesitate, do it now!

10. Contact your counselor and discuss slips in your aftercare session.

We have also provided a Clinical Vignette, demonstrating how to "process" a lapse with a patient.

Clinical Vignette

Clinical Discussion of a Lapse to Alcohol Use

Patient: So, the reason that I didn't come in last week was because I was too embarrassed to tell you that I had been drinking.

Therapist: Tell me more about that.

Patient: On Friday night, I went out with some friends after work. They wanted to go to a bar downtown. It had been a really tough week at work, and going out sounded fun. I know that one of my goals had been to avoid going to bars, but I really just wanted to just spend some down time with friends. One thing led to another, and the next thing I knew, I was too drunk to drive home. I had to call my husband to come pick me up.

Therapist: When you say, "One thing led to another," what happened, exactly?

Patient: Well, it was a bar where I used to drink all the time. I know the bartender there. He kept asking me why I didn't want a drink. My friends were pressuring me too. They were all drinking. And the week had been so stressful. I really wanted a drink. I thought it would help me to relax.

Therapist: You said that the next thing you knew, you were too drunk to drive home. How did you go from wanting one drink to being too drunk to drive home?

Patient: It was just all of my old patterns. One drink wasn't enough to even notice that I felt more relaxed. So I thought, "One more can't hurt anything." But when I had the second drink, I started feeling really good. For the first time that week I was actually happy. Since I felt good, all I wanted to do was to keep drinking.

Therapist: So, let's take one thing at a time. First of all, we've talked about how having a lapse is a normal part of the process of recovery.

Patient: I know. But I was doing so well and now I've ruined everything.

Therapist: You say that you've ruined everything. What is the evidence for that? Have you had anything else to drink since that Friday night?

Patient: Well, no, I haven't. But I just feel like by drinking once, I've taken several steps backward.

Therapist: It seems to me like you've been really strong to not let that one night lead you back to your old habits of drinking every day.

Patient: Okay. I guess that's true. But my husband is really upset with me.

Therapist: We can talk more about your husband's reaction to this event, but first, let's take a look at what happened that led you to drinking that night. Let's go back to breaking it down, step by step. And as we do that, I'd like you to think about some of the plans that you had in place, to help keep you from drinking.

Patient: Well, I guess I really should have resisted going to the bar in the first place. I know better than to hang out with the friends I used to drink with.

Therapist: That's a good start. It seems that both the place and the people were triggers for your drinking. What other triggers might there have been?

Patient: A bad week at work. Just feeling really drained.

Therapist: And, you mentioned that you were being pressured to drink. Both by your friends and by the bartender. It sounds like you went from a stressful situation at work to lots of pressures at the bar.

> **Clinical Vignette**
> **(Continued)**
>
> Patient: Yeah. I guess my resistance was really down.
> Therapist: Were there other things you could have done to feel better? Other places you could have gone or people you could have spent time with?
> Patient: My husband had been suggesting all week that we should plan a date night. Thinking back, dinner and a movie would have been a really nice way to spend a Friday evening. And if I had done that, he wouldn't be so angry with me.
> Therapist: It sounds to me like you still need that date night.
> Patient: I just need to convince him that I am serious about my recovery. Maybe I should talk to him about why I drank that night. And I haven't had a drink since it happened. I really am serious about not backtracking.
> Therapist: You are the only one that can keep yourself from backtracking. And you have a lot of tools to keep something like this from happening again. But there's one other thing. It's really important to come in for your sessions, even if you are embarrassed about something that has happened. That way, we can work through it together. Okay?

Concluding Comments on Relapse Prevention

We began our discussion of RP by noting that, in a sense, all alcohol treatment methods are designed to prevent relapse. Along these lines, what is more formally known as relapse prevention in the treatment field, cognitive behavioral therapy – relapse prevention, also may be and has been used as an adjunct with other, non-CBT treatment methods, such as 12-step approaches and pharmacotherapy. In this regard, a main reason for the rapid and wide dissemination of RP methods is that they brought attention and a proposed solution to the long discussed clinical problem of maintaining any changes in alcohol use that treatment may have helped to initiate. Accordingly, RP methods easily fit with a number of alcohol treatment methods that would not be called CBT-based. Another point about RP is that there sometimes is resistance among clinical staff to the idea that relapse is a normal or common part of the behavior change process. The objection to teaching patients this perspective is that it may give them "permission" to deviate from their stated goals of abstinence from or moderation in alcohol or other drug use. However, based on the now large volume of clinical research on the topic, RP methods seem to help individuals maintain the changes in alcohol or other drug use that may have been initiated voluntarily.

4.4   Psychopharmacological Methods

Pharmacotherapy can be a valuable treatment adjunct

In the United States, there are three medications or pharmacotherapies for AUDs that are approved by the U.S. Food and Drug Administration (FDA). These three medications, acamprosate, naltrexone, and disulfiram, also are the three medications that have at least some empirical support for the treatment of AUDs. Table 8 below presents the presumed mechanisms of action for each

Table 8
Empirically Supported Pharmacotherapy for AUDs and Presumed Mechanisms of Action

Medication	Mechanism
Acamprosate	Suppresses craving/urge to drink alcohol elicited by environmental cues.
Naltrexone	Reduces alcohol's rewarding effects by blocking effects of alcohol-released opioids in the brain.
Disulfiram (supervised)	Blocks metabolism of alcohol causing aversive physical reaction if alcohol is consumed.

of these medications. Our discussion of pharmacotherapy is based on an article by Lingford-Hughes, Welch, and Nutt (2004).

There are several points about the evidence for the clinical use of the empirically supported pharmacotherapies of AUDs. These medications have been evaluated in the context of their use as adjuncts to a psychosocial intervention with alcohol dependent patients whose goal is to abstain from alcohol. Therefore, they are used to promote abstinence and for relapse prevention. Again, this is readily apparent in our description of empirically supported psychosocial interventions such as BCT and CR. Strictly speaking, use of medication to treat AUDs follows a biological model of the etiology and treatment of the AUDs. However, the fact that the medications have been tested and used with psychosocial interventions reflects a biopsychosocial approach. In addition, the "empirical support" for the three medications comes primarily from research that compares a respective medication with a placebo. There is little evidence on the differential effectiveness of, say, naltrexone and acamprosate when the two drugs are compared directly with each other. Furthermore, the research on these medications has been done primarily with patients who are alcohol dependent, so there is not clear empirical support for their use with patients who have been identified as, say, hazardous drinkers or as alcohol abusers. Another point is that, since its introduction to the practice of alcohol treatment over 50 years ago, disulfiram's effectiveness has been limited by the degree to which patients comply with the prescribed regimen of taking it. The use of disulfiram is empirically supported only if its administration is monitored, as in an arrangement that is used as part of BCT's sobriety contract.

The research to date also has not answered several major questions regarding clinical application of AUD pharmacotherapies. First, it is not clear which patients are most likely to benefit from the use of which AUD medication. Second, it has not been shown that naltrexone or acamprosate is effective for individuals whose goal is moderate drinking rather than abstinence, or if these medications should continue to be prescribed once an individual has begun drinking after a period of abstinence. Third, it has not been firmly established whether psychosocial interventions are differentially effective when their use is combined with different medications. It is our position that any investigation of this question should begin with psychosocial interventions that have empirical support, such as the family of CBT interventions. In this regard, there is some evidence for the differential effectiveness of basic CBT combined with naltrexone compared to "supportive therapy" combined with naltrexone.

4.5   Mutual (Peer) Self-Help Groups

Involvement in self-help groups is an important component of the recovery process for many patients

The topic of mutual or self-help groups is included in the book because of their popularity and therefore importance in alcohol treatment. For example, Humphreys, et al. (2004) estimated that in the United States about 1.7 million men and women are members of addiction self-help groups. Despite their popularity, there actually is little empirical support based on randomized clinical trials or other experimental research for the efficacy or effectiveness of self-help groups. However, substantial observational or correlational research has been done on this topic, virtually all of it on the twelve-step program of Alcoholics Anonymous (AA). In recent years, the quality of this research has increased considerably, and it suggests that involvement in AA is associated with better outcomes (alcohol or other drug use, and functioning in other areas). Along these lines, in our clinical experience, twelve-step group involvement can be invaluable when used as part of an empirically-supported treatment, such as basic CBT or BCT (indeed these methods do include self-help group involvement as part of their approach to stabilize substance use or to prevent a lapse or relapse from occurring if abstinence is achieved). We see twelve-step group involvement's main value as aiding maintenance of change. In this regard, self-help groups are accessible and free of charge or subject only to voluntary donations for their use. As a result, they can be used as often as desired with few barriers to attendance and thus could be a major help to patients in their efforts to maintain the changes they may have initiated in treatment.

It is important to note that an intervention called twelve-step facilitation therapy (TSF; Nowinski, Baker, & Carroll, 1992) was one of the interventions tested as part of the alcohol treatment multisite clinical trial conducted in the United States in the early 1990s called Project MATCH. TSF showed little difference in outcomes in that trial when compared to motivational enhancement treatment and basic CBT. In addition, TSF was superior to either of the other two treatments on outcomes such as involvement in AA and continuous abstinence days during follow-up. Since Project MATCH's data were published in the late 1990s, TSF has shown efficacy in a few other trials and thus is considered to be an "empirically supported" alcohol treatment.

Before the last 20 years or so, the only self-help group options for patients desiring to change their patterns of alcohol use were AA and its twelve-step variants. Unfortunately, the emphasis on both lack of control (over alcohol) and spirituality that characterizes the twelve-step approach were not acceptable for some patients, and therefore their value as a part of a program of maintenance of changes in alcohol use could not be realized. In response to this problem, several alternatives to AA were created that countered the twelve step model with an emphasis on the individual's control over whether to drink or not (this does not mean that these groups support a goal of moderation or "controlled" drinking) and do not make any reference to a "higher power" or spirituality as part of their programs. Two of the more prominent examples of these alternative groups include Self-Management and Recovery Training (SMART) and Secular Organizations for Sobriety (SOS). Moderation Management (MM) is another mutual help group that uses a secular approach, but in contrast to most other mutual-help organizations, MM does not emphasize abstinence as the primary goal. As a result of the focus on moderation, individuals who affiliate with MM are less likely to be alcohol dependent and tend to be less impaired by their alcohol problems as compared to AA members (Humphreys & Klaw, 2001). Another distinctive characteristic of MM is the appeal to potential members using Internet-based mutual-help meetings. Although moderation-based approaches continue to be the source of some controversy, there is cause to believe that such programs fill a needed niche, and as such, provide a public health benefit (Humphreys, 2003). These alternative groups are not nearly as prevalent and therefore are not as accessible as AA is, but when available they do provide an option for individuals who are not receptive to AA's program of recovery. In addition, there is little empirical research on these alternative self-help groups, so it is impossible to say if involvement in them is associated with better functioning. On the other hand, it is expected that, as individuals use alternatives to AA, research on them will be generated.

At present there is not enough research on AA (or other self-help groups) to derive an empirically-based profile that clinicians can use to identify patients who most likely would benefit from attendance. Therefore, our general guidance is that clinicians introduce patients to the idea of self-help groups, identify the potential benefits, and then allow patients to decide whether to attend. We often encourage patients to attend several meetings so that they can form an impression of which aspects of the meetings may be beneficial to them. The clinician can then highlight any perceived benefits in terms of encouraging the patient to attend subsequent meetings.

4.6   Efficacy and Prognosis

We provided earlier, in Chapter 1, an overview of the prognosis associated with the treatment of alcohol use disorders (see Section 1.4). Here, we summarize current knowledge and evidence on the efficacy of the treatment approaches discussed earlier in this chapter. We are guided by the work of William Miller and his colleagues, who since the late 1970s have been regularly reviewing and updating alcohol treatment outcome studies. In their recent summary of the literature, Miller, Wilbourne, and Hettema (2003) evaluated 381 clinical trials that met their inclusion criteria, including the evaluation of a treatment designed to impact on an alcohol use disorder, the inclusion of a control or comparison condition, and a procedure to equate the participants in the groups being studied (e.g., randomization to treatment condition). For each study included in the review, a "cumulative evidence score" was calculated. Sufficient studies were available to calculate cumulative evidence scores for 47 different treatment approaches.

The efficacy of a number of treatment approaches for AUDs has been documented

The Miller et al. (2003) review identified 18 treatment modalities for which there was a positive cumulative evidence score, indicating overall support for the use of that modality across the studies evaluating it. Ranked first and second on the basis of cumulative evidence score were brief interventions and motivational enhancement, which we highlighted earlier in this chapter. Also receiving positive cumulative evidence scores were community reinforcement approaches and behavioral marital therapy. Several components of cognitive-behavioral therapy also received positive evidence scores, particularly behavioral contracting, social skills training, behavioral self-control training, and cognitive therapy. Finally, in the domain of pharmacological interventions, the use of acamprosate and naltrexone both received positive evidence scores. Disulfiram, the contemporary use of which is not widespread, received mixed support that on balance did not yield a positive cumulative evidence score.

Our review of treatment interventions included coverage of relapse prevention. As we noted, much of what falls under the heading of relapse prevention is cognitive-behavioral in nature, particularly the use of coping skills to avoid returns to drinking in high-risk situations. While various cognitive-behavioral aspects of relapse prevention received support in the Miller et al. (2003) review, the evidence in support of relapse prevention as a unique treatment modality was mixed. In contrast, another review of treatment interventions (McGovern & Carroll, 2003) found support for relapse prevention. Miller et al. do note that the studies on relapse prevention in their review included varying mixtures of cognitive-behavioral interventions, which may have contributed to the mixed findings.

Finally, it should be noted that study of Alcoholics Anonymous is a remarkably complex undertaking. Perhaps not surprisingly, the available data on the effectiveness of self-help groups broadly speaking are limited and mixed (McCrady, Horvath, & Delaney, 2003; Miller et al., 2003). While 12-step facilitation treatment has received some support (Project MATCH Research Group, 1997), this treatment as well warrants more systematic study.

4.7   Combination of Treatment Methods

Treatment often entails application of multiple treatment strategies

Each patient is unique; each will differ in the nature of his or her alcohol use disorder, the associated consequences, and the extent of supports and psychological resources available to draw upon in the treatment endeavor. The evaluation of these matters occurs in the assessment process and culminates in the development of the treatment plan. With the treatment goals thus articulated, the challenge is to match treatment strategies with the problems to be addressed. Often this will entail application of multiple strategies. For example, it is not uncommon to have patients attend several meetings of Alcoholics Anonymous to determine if that involvement holds benefit for the patient. Similarly, patients sometimes will be evaluated for adjunctive pharmacological agents. Either or both of these strategies might be used in the context of a broader treatment utilization of cognitive-behavioral treatment. The strongest guidance that can be offered on the combination of treatment methods is to select those interventions that have the greatest potential for ameliorating the presenting concerns of the patient, taking into account his or her unique circumstances.

4.8   Problems in Carrying Out Treatment

A variety of difficulties could potentially arise in the provision of clinical services with persons with alcohol use disorders. It is important to recognize and promptly address these difficulties if and when they arise.

One frequent problem found by clinicians is patient dropout from treatment. One strategy for addressing this is ensuring that patients understand what treatment entails, including discussion on what the therapist will expect from the patient and what the patient can expect on the part of the therapist. Research has shown that preparing patients for treatment increases session attendance, likely because ambiguity about the treatment process is reduced and motivation is enhanced.

Preparing patients for treatment and developing behavioral contracts regarding attendance can decrease treatment drop-out rates

Other strategies for reducing treatment dropout are available. Therapists can develop written behavioral contracts with patients that specify treatment attendance guidelines. Often these agreements will identify a time-limited course of attendance, at which time the patient and therapist can review progress to date and determine, as warranted, subsequent steps to be taken, including a renewal of the contract. Further, there may be value in including a "final session" clause in the contract, specifying that the patient will not cease treatment participation in the absence of a close-out session with the therapist.

Another difficulty often faced in treatment is low or inconsistent motivation to change, and patients sometimes will be discouraged when change is difficult or slow to materialize. These phenomena should be recognized and normalized. A challenge for the therapist is to work with the patient on maximizing motivation and commitment to change (recall the motivational interventions described earlier in this chapter). Similarly, efforts can be taken to instill and maintain hope and optimism on the part of the patient, especially when inevitable discouragements or setbacks occur.

While perhaps obvious, it is important for the therapist and patient to have similar ideas about treatment goals, tasks, and respective responsibilities. When there are differences in understanding about these parts of the treatment plan, the working alliance between the therapist and the patient will suffer, impeding progress and increasing the likelihood of treatment dropout.

4.9   Multicultural Considerations

Investigation into multicultural differences is one area that has received little attention in the literature on empirically supported treatment. As noted in Chapter 1, alcohol *abuse* is more prevalent among Whites than among Blacks, Asians, and Hispanics. Rates of alcohol *dependence* are more comparable across groups, although Whites, Native Americans, and Hispanics have higher rates of alcohol dependence than do Asians. Despite somewhat lower rates of AUDs among most minority groups, ethnic minority individuals are likely to experience higher levels of negative health and social consequences related to drinking, as compared to Whites (see Caetano, 2003). Further, there is some research suggesting that individuals from minority cultures are less likely to enter and remain in treatment programs. Thus, examination of treatment outcome among minority subgroups is of high priority, as evidenced by numerous recent initiatives calling for research on racial and ethnic disparities in health care.

Unfortunately, research findings are scarce with regard to treatment outcome from a multicultural perspective. Further, extant findings allow for limited interpretation, due to a number of biases in the existing research. Namely, (a) outcome findings may be attributable to inherent unidentified differences between ethnic groups, rather than to mechanisms of the treatment approach, (b) typical research exclusion criteria often differentially exclude minority patients from entering treatment outcome studies, (c) minority patients are less likely to enter and remain in treatment, which may result in only the most motivated minority patients being recruited into treatment outcome studies, and (d) any given ethnic or cultural designation is likely to be so broad as to include a heterogeneous mix of patients, which may mask meaningful between group differences (Schmidt, Greenfield, & Mulia, 2006). Aside from these limitations, there are limited data to suggest that despite the profound lack of attention toward gearing treatment approaches to address specific cultural needs, minority patients show comparable benefits from alcohol treatment as White patients. For example, results from the large multisite Project MATCH study suggest that ethnic minority participants had similar alcohol outcomes as compared to White participants (Tonigan, 2003). Project MATCH used three manual-guided treatments that were discussed earlier in this chapter: CBT, MET, and 12-step facilitation (TSF). At pretreatment, Whites, Blacks, and Hispanics had similar levels of alcohol involvement, alcohol-related consequences, and alcohol dependence, yet other pretreatment indicators favored the treatment success of White participants. Specifically, Blacks and Hispanics were less educated, had lower paying jobs, and were less likely to be married or cohabiting. In addition, Blacks and Hispanics attended fewer therapy sessions, reported less readiness to change behavior, and reported lower levels of satisfaction with treatment as compared to Whites. Despite these indicators that Black and Hispanic patients may fare less well in treatment, outcomes did not differ across the three groups on posttreatment measures of abstinent days, drinks per drinking day, and alcohol-related consequences. Moreover, in the outpatient subsample, Blacks reported less frequent drinking at 6 and 12 months posttreatment relative to Whites (Tonigan, 2003). In sum, although none of the treatments offered in Project MATCH were designed to be culturally sensitive, and despite the poor prognostic factors for Black and Hispanic participants, outcomes did not differ by ethnic or racial group.

A smaller, nonrandomized treatment study at an outpatient addiction treatment center similarly found no outcome differences for Blacks versus Whites, despite similar levels of problem severity for both groups (Brower & Carey, 2003). As with the Project MATCH study, Black participants in Brower and Carey's study had poorer pretreatment indicators including less likely to be employed, lower income, less likely to be married, lower educational attainment, and poorer physical health. Black participants received less treatment hours than White participants, yet outcomes were similar for both groups on reported reductions in number of days drinking and drinks per drinking day. The authors suggested that two factors favoring Black participants may have contributed to their success with treatment. Namely, Black participants indicated stronger social support for abstinence and were more likely to remain in the study as compared to White participants.

Some empirically supported treatments may show greater benefit than others for certain minority groups. For example, in the Project MATCH study, Native Americans were more likely to have positive outcomes in the MET condition as compared to the CBT or TSF conditions (Villanueva, Tonigan, & Miller, 2002). Again, differing benefits of particular treatment methods for specific minority groups have rarely been examined.

Treatments designed to be culturally sensitive may result in even more positive outcomes for ethnic minorities. As suggested by Schmidt et al. (2006), it is possible that tailoring treatment programs to the unique needs of different ethnic groups would result in greater success with the ongoing problem of engagement and retention of minority patients in alcohol treatment. As aptly summarized by Schmidt and colleagues, "Perhaps the most important, and humbling, conclusion to take from the literature is the realization of how inadequately the potential for racial and ethnic differences in quality, appropriateness, and effectiveness of care for alcohol problems has been explored" (2006, p. 53). Although limited guidance is available through the scant literature, researchers and clinicians alike should remain sensitive to cultural issues in the context of the process of treatment. We believe that thorough assessment and individualized treatment planning should result in treatment that is unique to the patient, and that should accordingly be sensitive to his or her cultural background.

5

Further Reading

Books

Center for Substance Abuse Treatment. (1999). *Enhancing motivation for change in substance abuse treatment*. Treatment Improvement Protocol (TIP) Series, No. 35. DHHS Pub. No. (SMA) 05–4081. Rockville, MD: Substance Abuse and Mental Health Services Administration. (Available free from CSAT: http://www.ncbi.nlm.nih.gov/books/bv.fcgi?rid=hstat5.chapter.61302).

This excellent monograph provides an overview of strategies designed to increase motivation for change among persons with substance use disorders.

Connors, G. J., Donovan, D. D., & DiClemente, C. C. (2001). *Substance abuse treatment and the stages of change*. New York: Guilford Press.

This volume provides a comprehensive and user-friendly guide to the application of the stages of change model in alcohol and drug abuse treatment.

Marlatt, G. A., & Donovan, D. D. (Eds.) (2005). *Relapse prevention: Maintenance strategies in the treatment of addictive behaviors* (2nd ed.). New York: Guilford Press.

This book is an excellent resource for understanding the nature of relapse and for preparing patients for avoiding or otherwise coping with situations that present high-risk for relapse.

Meyers, R. K., & Smith, J. E. (1995). *Clinical guide to alcohol treatment: The community reinforcement approach*. New York: Guilford Press.

The community reinforcement approach is fully delineated in this volume, along with relevant clinical techniques and strategies designed to apply the approach.

Miller, W. R., & Rollnick, S. (2002). *Motivational interviewing: Preparing people for change* (2nd ed.). New York: Guilford Press.

This book provides excellent coverage on motivational interviewing, a now widely-used clinical strategy for overcoming the ambivalence that often is an obstacle to achieving behavioral change.

O'Farrell, T. J., & Fals-Stewart, W. (2006). *Behavioral couples therapy for alcoholism and drug abuse*. New York: Guilford Press.

This volume provides a practical, hands-on guide to the conduct of behavioral couples therapy.

Rollnick, S., Mason, P., & Butler, C. (1999). *Health behavior change*. New York: Elsevier.

Written for health professionals, this guide for practitioners provides counselors with a host of readily-applicable strategies for productively working with patients seeking to make changes in their behavior.

Sobell, M. B., & Sobell, L. C. (1993). *Problem drinkers: Guided self-change treatment*. New York: Guilford Press.

This user-friendly guide for practitioners provides a structured approach for working with problem drinkers.

Washton, A. M., & Zweben, J. E. (2006). *Treating alcohol and drug problems in psychotherapy practice*. New York: Guilford Press.

This very useful book presents an integrated model for addressing substance use disorders within an office-based practice environment.

Websites

For Patients

Software to assist with moderating drinking (Behavior Therapy Associates; Reid Hester)
    http://www.selfhelpmagazine.com/about/staff/software.html
Self-Help Magazine: Alcohol, Tobacco, & Other Drugs
    http://www.selfhelpmagazine.com/articles/atd/index.shtml
Drinker's Check-Up (Reid Hester)
    http://www.drinkerscheckup.com
Smart Recovery
    http://www.smartrecovery.org
Moderation Management
    http://www.moderation.org
Alcoholics Anonymous (official website)
    http://www.alcoholics-anonymous.org
Secular Organizations for Sobriety
    http://www.secularsobriety.org
Alcohol Screening.org
    http://www.alcoholscreening.org

For Practitioners

Cancer Prevention Resource Center (home of the Transtheoretical Model; James Prochaska)
    http://www.uri.edu/research/cprc/about-us.htm
Center on Alcoholism, Substance Abuse, and Addictions (William Miller)
    http://casaa.unm.edu
World Health Organization, Management of Substance Abuse
    http://www.who.int/substance_abuse/en
NIAAA Professional Education Materials
    http://www.niaaa.nih.gov/Publications/EducationTrainingMaterials/default.htm
Project Mainstream – Improving Substance Abuse Education for Health Professionals
    http://www.projectmainstream.net
Alcohol and Health – Boston Medical Center, Boston University
    http://www.bu.edu/act/alcoholandhealth/index.html
Addiction Technology Transfer Center
    http://www.nattc.org/index.html
NIAAA – Helping Patients Who Drink Too Much: A Clinician's Guide
    http://pubs.niaaa.nih.gov/publications/Practitioner/CliniciansGuide2005/clinicians_guide.htm
NIAAA – Assessing Alcohol Problems: A Guide for Clinicians and Researchers
    http://pubs.niaaa.nih.gov/publications/Assesing%20Alcohol/index.htm

For Patients and Practitioners

Guided Self-Change Clinic
    http://www.nova.edu/gsc
NIAAA Fact Sheets, Pamphlets, Brochures, and Posters
    http://www.niaaa.nih.gov/Publications/PamphletsBrochuresPosters/English
Center for Substance Abuse Treatment (includes a facility locator)
    http://csat.samhsa.gov

6

References

Allen, J. P., Sillanaukee, P., Strid, N., & Litten, R. Z. (2003). Biomarkers of heavy drinking. In J. P. Allen & V. B. Wilson (Eds.), *Assessing alcohol problems* (2nd ed.) (pp. 37–53). Bethesda, MD: National Institutes of Health.

Allen, J. P., & Wilson, V. B. (Eds.). (2003). *Assessing alcohol problems: A guide for clinicians and researchers* (2nd Ed.). Bethesda, MD: National Institutes of Health. Available at http://pubs.niaaa.nih.gov/publications/Assesing%20Alcohol/index.htm.

American Psychiatric Association. (1994). *Diagnostic and statistical manual of mental disorders* (4th ed.). Washington, DC: American Psychiatric Association.

American Psychiatric Association. (2000). *Diagnostic and statistical manual of mental disorders* (4th ed., text revision). Washington, DC: American Psychiatric Association.

Annis, H. M. (1987). *Situational Confidence Questionnaire*. Toronto: Addiction Research Foundation.

Annis, H. M., & Graham, J. M. (1988). *Situational Confidence Questionnaire user's guide*. Toronto: Addiction Research Foundation.

Annis, H. M., & Martin, G. (1985). *Inventory of drug-taking situations*. Toronto: Addiction Research Foundation.

Annis, H. M., Turner, N. E., & Sklar, S. M. (1997). *Inventory of drug-taking situations: User's guide*. Toronto: Addiction Research Foundation, Centre for Addiction and Mental Health.

Babor, T. F. (1994). Avoiding the horrid and healthy sin of drunkenness: Does dissuasion make a difference? *Journal of Consulting and Clinical Psychology, 62*, 1127–1140.

Bandura, A. (1969). *Principles of behavior modification*. Englewood Cliffs, NJ: Prentice Hall.

Bandura, A. (1977). *Social learning theory*. Englewood Cliffs, NJ: Prentice Hall.

Bandura, A. (1986). *Social foundations of thought and action: A social cognitive theory*. Englewood Cliffs, NJ: Prentice Hall.

Bien, T. H., Miller, W. R., & Tonigan, J. S. (1993). Brief interventions for alcohol problems: A review. *Addiction, 88*, 315–336.

Breslin, F. C., Sobell, L. C., Sobell, M. B., & Agrawal, S. (2000). A comparison of a brief and long version of the Situational Confidence Questionnaire. *Behvior Research and Therapy, 38*, 1211–1220.

Brower, K. J., & Carey, T. L. (2003). Racially related health disparities and alcoholism treatment outcomes. *Alcoholism: Clinical and Experimental Research, 27*, 1365–1367.

Caetano, R. (2003). Alcohol-related health disparities and treatment-related epidemiological findings among Whites, Blacks, and Hispanics in the United States. *Alcoholism: Clinical and Experimental Research, 27*, 1337–1339.

Carey, K. B., & Maisto, S. A. (2006). *Motivational interviewing for patients with co-occurring substance abuse and mental illness*. Invited workshop presented at Hutchings Psychiatric Center, Department of Psychiatry, SUNY Upstate Medical University, Syracuse, NY January.

Carey, K. B., Purnine, D. M., Maisto, S. A., & Carey, M. P. (1999). Assessing readiness to change substance abuse: A critical review of instruments. *Clinical Psychology: Science and Practice, 6*, 245–266.

Carroll, K. M. (1998). *A cognitive-behavioral approach: Treating cocaine addiction*. Rockville, MD: National Institute on Drug Abuse.

Center for Substance Abuse Treatment. (1999). *Enhancing motivation for change in substance abuse treatment*. Treatment Improvement Protocol (TIP) Series, No. 35. DHHS Pub. No. (SMA) 05–4081. Rockville, MD: Substance Abuse and Mental Health Services Administration.

Connors, G. J., Longabaugh, R., & Miller, W. R. (1996). Looking forward and back to relapse: Implications for research and practice. *Addiction, 91*(Supplement), 191–196.

Davidson, R. (1998). The transtheoretical model: A critical overview. In W. R. Miller & N. Heather (Eds.), *Treating addictive behaviors* (2nd ed.) (pp. 25–38). New York: Plenum.

Dawson, D. A., Grant, B. F., Stinson, F., Chou, P. S., Huang, B., & Juan, W. J. (2005). Recovery from DSM-IV alcohol dependence: United States, 2001–2002. *Addiction, 100*, 281–292.

DiClemente, C. C., Carbonari, J. P., Montgomery, R. P. G., & Hughes, S. O. (1994). The Alcohol Abstinence Self-Efficacy Scale. *Journal of Studies on Alcohol, 55*, 141–148.

Donovan, D. M. (1988). Assessment of addictive behaviors: Implications of an emerging biopsychosocial model. In D. M. Donovan & G. A. Marlatt (Eds.), *Assessment of addictive behaviors* (pp. 3–48). New York: Guilford Press.

Donovan, D. M. (2005). Assessment of addictive behaviors for relapse prevention. In D. M. Donovan & G. A. Marlatt (Eds.), *Assessment of addictive behaviors* (2nd ed.) (pp. 1–48). New York: Guilford Press.

Donovan D. M., & Marlatt G. A. (Eds.). (2005), *Assessment of addictive behaviors*. New York: Guilford Press.

Edwards, G., & Gross, M.M. (1976). Alcohol dependence: Provisional description of a clinical syndrome. *British Medical Journal, 1*, 1058–1061.

Engel, G. L. (1977). The need for a new medical model: A challenge for biomedicine. *Science, 196*, 129–136.

Engel, G. L. (1980). The clinical application of the biopsychosocial model. *American Journal of Psychiatry, 137*, 535–544.

Finney, J. W., Moos, R. H., & Timko, C. (1999). The course of treated and untreated substance use disorders: Remission and resolution, relapse and mortality. In B. S. McCrady & E. E. Epstein (Eds.), *Addictions: A comprehensive guidebook* (pp. 30–49). New York: Oxford University Press.

Folkman, S., & Lazarus, R. S. (1988). *Ways of Coping Questionnaire* (Research ed.) Redwood City, CA: Consulting Psychologists Press, Inc.

Gonzalez, V. M., Schmitz, J. M., & DeLaune, K. A. (2006). The role of homework in cognitive-behavioral therapy for cocaine dependence. *Journal of Consulting and Clinical Psychology, 74*, 633–637.

Grant, B. F. (1997). Prevalence and correlates of alcohol use and DSM-IV alcohol dependence in the United States: Results of the National Longitudinal Alcohol Epidemiologic Survey. *Journal of Studies on Alcohol, 58*, 464–473.

Grant, B. F., & Dawson, D. A. (1999). Alcohol and drug use, abuse, and dependence: Classification, prevalence, and comorbidity. In B. S. McCrady & E. E. Epstein (Eds.), *Addictions: A comprehensive guidebook* (pp. 9–29). New York: Oxford University Press.

Grant, B. F., Dawson, D. A., Stinson, F. S., Chou, S. P., Dufour, M. C., & Pickering, R. P. (2004). The 12-month prevalence and trends in DSM-IV alcohol abuse and dependence: United States, 1991–1992 and 2001–2002. *Drug and Alcohol Dependence, 74*, 223–234.

Guyatt, G. (1992). Critical evaluation of radiologic technologies. *Canadian Association of Radiologists Journal, 43*, 6–7.

Higgins, S. T., & Petry, N. M. (1999). Contingency management. *Alcohol Research and Health, 23*, 122–127.

Humphreys, K. (2003). A research-based analysis of the Moderation Management controversy. *Psychiatric Services, 54*, 621–622.

Humphreys, K., & Klaw, E. (2001). Can targeting nondependent problem drinkers and providing internet-based services expand access to assistance for alcohol problems?

A study of the Moderation Management self-help/mutual aid organization. *Journal of Studies on Alcohol*, *62*, 528–532.

Humphreys, K., Wing, S., McCarty, D., Chappel, J., Gallant, L., Haberle, B., et al. (2004). Self-help organizations for alcohol and drug problems: Toward evidence-based practice and policy. *Journal of Substance Abuse Treatment*, *26*, 151–158.

Institute of Medicine. (1990). *Alcohol problems*. Washington, DC: National Academies Press.

Institute of Medicine. (2001). *Primary care*. Washington, DC: National Academies Press.

Kazantzis, N., Deane, F. P., & Ronan, K. R. (2000). Homework assignments in cognitive and behavioral therapy: A meta-analysis. *Clinical Psychology: Science and Practice*, *7*, 189–202.

Kazantzis, N., Deane, F. P., & Ronan, K. R. (2004). Assessing compliance with homework assignments: Review and recommendations for clinical practice. *Journal of Clinical Psychology*, *60*, 627–641.

Kazantzis, N., Deane, F. P., Ronan, K. R., & L'Abate, L. (2005). *Using homework assignments in cognitive-behavioral therapy*. New York: Routledge.

Levant, R. F. (2004). The empirically validated treatments movement: A practitioner/educator perspective. *Clinical Psychology: Science and Practice*, *11*, 219–224.

Lingford-Hughes, A. R., Welch, S., & Nutt, D. J. (2004). Evidence-based guidelines for the pharmacological management of substance misuse, addiction, and comorbidity: Recommendations from the British Association for Psychopharmacology. *Journal of Psychopharmacology*, *18*, 293–335.

Litman, G. K., Stapleton, J., Oppenheim, A. N., & Peleg, M. (1983). An instrument for measuring coping behaviors in hospitalized alcoholics: Implications for relapse prevention and treatment. *British Journal of Addiction*, *78*, 269–276.

Litman, G. K., Stapleton, J., Oppenheim, A. N., Peleg, M., & Jackson, P. (1984). The relationship between coping behaviors and their effectiveness and alcoholism relapse and survival. *British Journal of Addiction*, *79*, 283–291.

Maisto, S. A., McKay, J. R., & Tiffany, S. T. (2003). Diagnosis. In J. P. Allen & V. B. Wilson (Eds.), *Assessing alcohol problems* (2nd ed.) (pp. 55–74). Bethesda, MD: National Institutes of Health.

Marlatt, G. A., & Donovan, D. M. (Eds.). (2005). *Relapse prevention: Maintenance strategies in the treatment of addictive behaviors* (2nd ed.). New York: Guilford Press.

Marlatt, G. A., & Gordon, J. (1980). Determinants of relapse: Implications for the maintenance of behavior change. In P. O. Davidson & S. M. Davidson (Eds.), *Behavior medicine: Changing health lifestyles* (pp. 410–452). New York: Bunner/Mazel.

Marlatt, G. A., & Gordon, J. (Eds.). (1985). *Relapse prevention*. New York: Guilford Press.

Marlatt, G. A., & Witkiewitz, K. (2005) Relapse prevention for alcohol and drug problems. In G. A. Marlatt & D. M. Donovan (Eds.), *Relapse prevention* (2nd ed.) (pp. 1–44). New York: Guilford Press.

McCrady, B. S., Horvath, A. T., & Delaney, S. I. (2003). Self-help groups. In R. K. Hester & W.R. Miller (Eds.), *Handbook of alcoholism treatment approaches: Effective alternatives* (3rd ed.) (pp. 165–187). Boston: Allyn and Bacon.

McCrady, B. S., Noel, N. E., Abrams, D. B., Stout, R. L., Nelson, H. F., & Hay, W. F. (1986). Comparative effectiveness of three types of spouse involvement in outpatient behavioral alcoholism treatment. *Journal of Studies on Alcohol*, *47*, 459–467.

McGovern, M. P., & Carroll, K. M. (2003). Evidence-based practice for substance use disorders. *Psychiatric Clinics of North America*, *26*, 991–1010.

McGovern, M. P., Fox, T. S., Xie, H., & Drake, R. E. (2004). A survey of clinical practices and readiness to adopt evidence-based practices: Dissemination research in an addiction research system. *Journal of Substance Abuse Treatment*, *26*, 305–312.

Meyers, R. J., & Smith, J. E. (1995). *Clinical guide to alcohol treatment: The community reinforcement approach*. New York: Guilford Press.

Meyers, R. J., Villanueva, M., & Smith, J. E. (2005). The community reinforcement approach: History and new directions. *Journal of Cognitive Psychotherapy*, *19*, 247–260.

Miller, W. R., Benefield, R. G., & Tonigan, J. S. (1993). Enhancing motivation for change in problem drinking: A controlled comparison of two therapist styles. *Journal of Consulting and Clinical Psychology, 61,* 455–461.

Miller, W. R., Heather, N., & Hall, W. (1991). Calculating standard drink units: International comparisons. *British Journal of Addiction, 86,* 43–47.

Miller, W. R., & Hester, R. K. (2003). Treating alcohol problems: Toward an informed eclectism. In R. K. Hester & W. R. Miller (Eds.), *Handbook of alcoholism treatment approaches: Effective alternatives* (3rd ed.) (pp. 1–12). Boston: Allyn & Bacon.

Miller, W. R., & Rollnick, S. (Eds.) (2002). *Motivational interviewing* (2nd ed.). New York: Guilford Press.

Miller, W. R., Tonigan, S., & Longabaugh, R. (1995). *The Drinker Inventory of Consequences (DrInC): An instrument for assessing adverse consequence of alcohol abuse.* NIAAA Project MATCH Monograph Series, Vol. 4 Washington, DC: Government Printing Office.

Miller, W. R., Walters, S. T., & Bennett, M. E. (2001). How effective is alcoholism treatment in the United States? *Journal of Studies on Alcohol, 62,* 211–220.

Miller, W. R., Wilbourne, P. L., & Hettema, J. E. (2003). What works? A summary of alcohol treatment outcome research. In R. K. Hester & W. R. Miller (Eds.), *Handbook of alcoholism treatment approaches: Effective alternatives* (3rd ed.) (pp. 13–63). Boston: Allyn and Bacon.

Monti, P. M., Abrams, D. B., Kadden, R. M., & Cooney, N. L. (1989). *Treating alcohol dependence: A coping skills training guide.* New York: Guilford Press.

Monti, P. M., Kadden, R. M., Rohsenow, D. J., Cooney, N. L., & Abrams, D. B. (2002). *Treating alcohol dependence: A coping skills training guide* (2nd ed.). New York: Guilford Press.

Moos, R. H. (1995). Development and application of new measures of life stressors, social resources, and coping responses. *European Journal of Psychological Assessment, 11,* 1–13.

Morgenstern, J., & Longabaugh, R. (2000). Cognitive-behavioral treatment for alcohol dependence: A review of evidence for its hypothesized mechanisms of action. *Addiction, 95,* 1475–1490.

National Institute on Alcohol Abuse and Alcoholism. (2005). *Helping patients who drink too much: A clinician's guide (2005 ed.).* NIH Pub No. 05–3769. Bethesda, MD: U.S. Department of Health and Human Services. Retrieved February 8, 2007, from http://pubs.niaaa.nih.gov/publications/Practitioner/CliniciansGuide2005/clinicians_guide.htm.

National Institute on Alcohol Abuse and Alcoholism. (2007). *What is a safe level of drinking?* In *FAQs for the general public- English.* Retrieved February 8, 2007 from http://www.niaaa.nih.gov/FAQs/General-English/FAQs13.htm.

Nowinski, J., Baker, S., & Carroll, K. (1992). *Twelve step facilitation therapy manual: A clinical research guide for therapists treating individuals with alcohol abuse and dependence.* NIAAA Project MATCH Monograph Series, Vol. 1 Washington, DC: Government Printing Office.

O'Brien, C. P. (2001). Drug addiction and drug abuse. In J. G. Hardman & L. E. Limbird (Eds.), *Goodman and Gilman's: The pharmacological basis of therapeutics* (10th ed.) (pp. 621–643). New York: McGraw-Hill.

O'Farrell, T. J., & Fals-Stewart, W. (2000). Behavioral couples therapy for alcoholism and drug abuse. *Journal of Substance Abuse Treatment, 18,* 51–54.

O'Farrell, T. J., & Fals-Stewart, W. (2002). Behavioral couples and family therapy for substance abusers. *Current Psychiatry Reports, 4,* 371–376.

O'Farrell, T. J., & Fals-Stewart, W. (2003). Marital and family therapy. In R. K. Hester & W. R. Miller (Eds.), *Handbook of alcoholism treatment approaches: Effective alternatives* (3rd ed.) (pp. 188–212). Boston: Allyn & Bacon.

Prochaska, J. O., DiClemente, C. C., & Norcross, J. J. C. (1992). In search of how people change. *American Psychologist, 47,* 1102–1114.

Project MATCH Research Group. (1997). Matching alcoholism treatments to client heterogeneity: Project MATCH posttreatment drinking outcomes. *Journal of Studies on Alcohol, 58,* 7–29.

Rollnick, S., Mason, P., & Butler, C. (1999). Health behavior change. New York: Elsevier.

Rush, A. J. (Ed.) (2000). *Handbook of psychiatric measures*. Washington, DC: American Psychiatric Press.

Saunders, J. B., Aasland, O. G., Babor, T. F., DeLaFuente, J. R., & Grant, M. (1993). Development of the Alcohol Use Disorders Identification Test (AUDIT): WHO collaborative project on early detection of persons with harmful alcohol consumption. *Addiction, 88*, 791–804.

Schmidt, L., Greenfield, T., & Mulia, N. (2006). Unequal treatment: Racial and ethnic disparities in alcoholism treatment services. *Alcohol Research and Health, 29*, 49–54.

Schonfeld, L., Peters, R., & Dolente, A. (1993). *SARA: Substance Abuse Relapse Assessment: Professional manual*. Odessa, FL: Psychological Assessment Resources.

Schuckit, M. A., Anthenelli, R. M., Bucholz, K. K., Hesselbrock, V. M., & Tipp, J. (1995). The time course of development of alcohol-related problems in men and women. *Journal of Studies on Alcohol, 56*, 218–225.

Schuckit, M. A., Daeppen, J. B., Tipp, J. E., Hesselbrock, M., & Bucholz, K. K. (1998). The clinical course of alcohol-related problems in alcohol dependent and nonalcohol dependent drinking women and men. *Journal of Studies on Alcohol, 59*, 581–590.

Schuckit, M. A., Smith, T. L., Danko, G. P., Bucholz, K. K., Reich, T., & Bierut, L. (2001). Five-year clinical course associated with DSM-IV alcohol abuse or dependence in a large group of men and women. *American Journal of Psychiatry, 158*, 1084–1090.

Shaffer, H. J., LaPlante, D. A., LaBrie, R. A., Kidman, R. C., Donato, A. N., & Stanton, M. V. (2004). Toward a syndrome model of addiction: Multiple expressions, common etiology. *Harvard Review of Psychiatry, 12*, 267–274.

Singleton, E. G. (1997). Alcohol Craving Questionnaire (ACQ-NOW). *Alcohol and Alcoholism, 32*, 344.

Sobell, L. C., Agrawal, S., & Sobell, M. B. (1999). Utility of liver function tests for screening "alcohol abusers" who are not severely dependent on alcohol. *Substance Use and Misuse, 34*, 1723–1732.

Sobell, L. C., Cunningham, J. A., & Sobell, M. B. (1996). Recovery from alcohol problems with and without treatment: Prevalence in two population surveys. *American Journal of Public Health, 86*, 966–972.

Sobell, L. C., Cunningham, J. A., Sobell, M. B., Agrawal, S., Gavin, D. R., Leo, G. I. et al. (1996). Fostering self-change among problem drinkers: A proactive community intervention. *Addictive Behaviors, 21*, 817–833.

Sobell, L. C., & Sobell, M. B. (1992). Timeline follow-back: A technique for assessing self-reported ethanol consumption. In J. Allen & R. Litten (Eds.), *Techniques to assess alcohol consumption* (pp. 41–72). Clifton, NJ: Humana Press.

Sobell, L. C., & Sobell, M. B. (2003). Assessment of drinking behavior. In J. P. Allen & V. B. Wilson (Eds.), *Assessing alcohol problems* (2nd ed.) (pp. 75–100). Bethesda, MD: National Institutes of Health.

Sobell, M. B., & Sobell, L. C. (2000). Stepped care as a heuristic approach to the treatment of alcohol problems. *Journal of Consulting and Clinical Psychology, 68*, 573–579.

Substance Abuse and Mental Health Services Administration. (2005). *2005 National Survey on Drug Use and Health: Detailed tables*. U.S. Department of Health and Human Services. Retrieved January 26, 2007 from http://oas.samhsa.gov/nsduh/2k5nsduh/tabs/sect2petabs1to57.htm.

Sutton, S. (1996). Can "stages of change" provide guidance in the treatment of addictions? A critical examination of Prochaska and DiClemente's model. In G. Edwards & C. Dare (Eds.), *Psychotherapy, psychological treatments and the addictions* (pp. 189–205). New York: Cambridge University Press.

Tonigan, J. S. (2003). Project Match treatment participation and outcome by self-reported ethnicity. *Alcoholism: Clinical and Experimental Research, 27*, 1340–1344.

Vaillant, G. E. (1983). *The natural history of alcoholism: Causes, patterns, and paths to recovery*. Cambridge, MA: Harvard University Press.

Villanueva, M., Tonigan, J. S., & Miller, W. R. (2002). A retrospective study of client-treatment matching: Differential treatment response of Native American alcoholics in

Project MATCH. *Alcoholism: Clinical and Experimental Research, 26*(Supplement*)*, 83A.

West, R. (2005). Time for a change: Putting the transtheoretical (stages of change) model to rest. *Addiction, 100*, 1036–1039.

Whitlock, E. P., Polen, M. R., Green, C. A., Orleans, T., Klein, J. (2004). Behavioral counseling interventions in primary care to reduce risky/harmful alcohol use by adults: A summary of the evidence for the U.S. Preventive Services Task Force. *Annals of Internal Medicine, 140*, 557–568.

Witkiewitz, K., Marlatt, G. A., & Walker, D. (2005). Mindfulness-based relapse prevention for alcohol and substance use disorders. *Journal of Cognitive Psychotherapy, 19*, 211–228.

World Health Organization (WHO). (1992). *International classification of diseases and related health problems* (10th revision). Geneva, Switzerland: WHO.

World Health Organization (WHO). (2004). *Global status report on alcohol – 2004*. Geneva, Switzerland: WHO.

7

Appendix: Tools and Resources

7.1   Overview

This appendix includes several forms that can be used in the assessment and treatment of alcohol use disorders. We have used these forms in a number of our treatment studies, and have found them to be clinically useful in our treatment activities.

7.2   Short Inventory of Problems (SIP)

The SIP (Miller, Tonigan, & Longabaugh, 1995) is a brief inventory of negative consequences associated with past alcohol use. The version provided here was developed to assess such problems using a lifetime perspective. It can be altered to assess other time periods of interest, such as the past 90 days or the past year. The measure is often used clinically to identify the nature and extent of drinking-related consequences, and to review these consequences with the patient.

7.3   Decisional Balance – The Pros and Cons of Drinking and of Quitting

This worksheet can be used by patients to identify the advantages and disadvantages of drinking and of quitting drinking. The information gathered can be used to conduct a decisional balance exercise in which the relative weightings of the advantages and disadvantages of change can be assessed.

7.4   Readiness Ruler

This readiness ruler can be used to assess a patient's current readiness to change his or her drinking. The ruler can be used to assess either readiness to quit or to reduce drinking (or to change other types of behaviors), and it can be administered on multiple occasions over time (e.g., at the beginning or end of each treatment session).

7.5   Alcohol Abstinence Self-Efficacy Scale (AASE)

The AASE (DiClemente, Carbonari, Montgomery, & Hughes, 1994) measures temptation to drink and confidence to abstain from drinking across a variety of situations. Participants answer each of the 20 questions twice, once to indicate temptation, the other to indicate efficacy to abstain.

Scores are calculated by adding the items in parentheses to obtain a score for each of the following 4 scales (for each efficacy and temptation): Negative Affect (3, 6, 14, 16, 18), Social/Positive (4, 8, 15, 17, 20), Physical and Other Concerns (2, 5, 9, 12, 13), Craving and Urges (1, 7, 10, 11, 19). Higher scores on the scales indicate greater efficacy (or temptation) related to those types of situations.

7.6   Daily Drinking Diary

It is often useful to have patients monitor their drinking on a daily basis. This form, which patients can complete each day between treatment sessions, provides information on when patients drink, situational information (such as the location, who else is present, thoughts/cognitions operating, mood), the amount of alcohol consumed, and consequences associated with the drinking. The form can be modified to assess other dimensions, such as the recording of temptations to drink. The information provided through use of the diary can be used in the conduct of a functional analysis of the patient's drinking and in the identification of high-risk for drinking situations.

7.7   Worksheet for Functional Analysis of Drinking Behavior

This worksheet can be used in performing a functional analysis of a patient's drinking behavior. Patients along or in collaboration with the therapist can complete the form with the goal of identifying the antecedents of drinking, the parameters of the actual drinking behavior, and the consequences (both short-term as well as long-term).

7.8   Alcohol Use Disorders Identification Test (AUDIT)

The AUDIT (Saunders, Aasland, Babor, DeLaFuente, & Grant, 1993) is a brief and efficient questionnaire available for use in assessing for a drinking problem. The scoring and interpretation of the measure are as follows:

Questions 1–8 are scored 0, 1, 2, 3, or 4 (with higher scores accorded to responses reflecting greater drinking or more frequent consequences). Questions 9 and 10 are scored 0, 2, or 4 only. The minimum score is 0 (for nondrinkers) and the maximum possible score is 40. A score of 8 or more indicates a strong likelihood of hazardous or harmful alcohol consumption.

7.9   Past Month Alcohol Use

We have provided pie charts for men and women, showing past month alcohol use by category (no use, some use, binge use, and heavy use). These charts can be used to provide feedback to patients regarding how their alcohol use compares to others' drinking.

7.10   High-Risk for Drinking Situations – Identification and Coping Strategies

This worksheet can be used by patients to list situations that have been associated with previous drinking or situations that the patient believes represent a risk for drinking in the future. A high-risk situation is defined as any event, thought, situation, place, or person potentially associated with risk for drinking. The patient can then identify coping strategies that can be used when faced with a high risk for drinking situation. The worksheet is especially useful in the context of relapse prevention.

7.11   What To Do if a Relapse Occurs

Drinking relapses often occur, especially during the early stages of treatment. It is important for patients to be prepared to face such situations, and also to be prepared to deal with relapses if they occur. Patients can use this handout to provide a course of action should they experience a relapse.

Short Inventory of Problems (SIP)

Here are a number of events that people sometimes experience. Read each one carefully, and circle YES or NO to indicate whether this has *EVER* happened to you. If an item does not apply to you, circle NO.

Has this *EVER* happened to you?

1.	I have been unhappy because of my drinking.	NO	YES
2.	Because of my drinking, I have not eaten properly.	NO	YES
3.	I have failed to do what is expected of me because of my drinking.	NO	YES
4.	I have felt guilty or ashamed because of my drinking.	NO	YES
5.	I have taken foolish risks when I have been drinking.	NO	YES
6.	When drinking, I have done impulsive things that I regretted later.	NO	YES
7.	My physical health has been harmed by my drinking.	NO	YES
8.	I have had money problems because of my drinking.	NO	YES
9.	My physical appearance has been harmed by my drinking.	NO	YES
10.	My family has been hurt by my drinking.	NO	YES
11.	A friendship or close relationship has been damaged by my drinking.	NO	YES
12.	My drinking has gotten in the way of my growth as a person.	NO	YES
13.	My drinking has damaged my social life, popularity, or reputation.	NO	YES
14.	I have spent too much or lost a lot of money because of my drinking.	NO	YES
15.	I have had an accident while drinking or intoxicated.	NO	YES

From: S.A. Maisto, G.J. Connors, & R.L. Dearing: *Alcohol Use Disorders*   © 2007 Hogrefe & Huber Publishers

Decisional Balance – The Pros and Cons of Drinking and of Quitting

One thing that helps people when thinking of changing is to list the benefits and costs of changing or continuing their current behavior. Completing this exercise will help you to think about the costs (cons) and benefits (pros) of changing and the issues that are involved in your decision to change your drinking. In order to make a change, the scale needs to tip so that the benefits outweigh the costs.

List below the pros, or advantages, of drinking.

List below the cons, or disadvantages, of drinking.

List below the pros, or advantages, of quitting drinking.

List below the cons, or disadvantages, of quitting drinking.

From: S.A. Maisto, G.J. Connors, & R.L. Dearing: *Alcohol Use Disorders*   © 2007 Hogrefe & Huber Publishers

Readiness Ruler

On the ruler shown below, please circle the number that best describes how you feel right now.

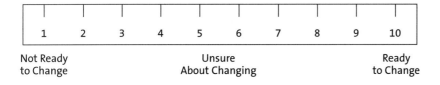

| 1 | 2 | 3 | 4 | 5 | 6 | 7 | 8 | 9 | 10 |

Not Ready
to Change

Unsure
About Changing

Ready
to Change

From: S.A. Maisto, G.J. Connors, & R.L. Dearing: *Alcohol Use Disorders*   © 2007 Hogrefe & Huber Publishers

Alcohol Abstinence Self-Efficacy Scale (AASE)

Listed below are a number of situations that lead some people to drink. We would first like to know how tempted you may be to drink in each of these situations. Please circle the number in each column that best describes your feelings of *temptation to drink* in each situation *at the present time* according to the 1 to 5 scale provided.

SITUATION	TEMPTED				
	Not at all	Not very	Moderately	Very	Extremely
1. When I am in agony because of stopping or withdrawing from alcohol use.	1	2	3	4	5
2. When I have a headache.	1	2	3	4	5
3. When I am feeling depressed.	1	2	3	4	5
4. When I am on vacation and want to relax.	1	2	3	4	5
5. When I am concerned about someone.	1	2	3	4	5
6. When I am very worried.	1	2	3	4	5
7. When I have the urge to try just one drink to see what happens.	1	2	3	4	5
8. When I am being offered a drink in a social situation.	1	2	3	4	5
9. When I dream about taking a drink.	1	2	3	4	5
10. When I want to test my willpower over drinking.	1	2	3	4	5
11. When I am feeling a physical need or craving for alcohol.	1	2	3	4	5
12. When I am physically tired.	1	2	3	4	5
13. When I am experiencing some physical pain or injury.	1	2	3	4	5
14. When I feel like blowing up because of frustration.	1	2	3	4	5
15. When I see others drinking at a bar or at a party.	1	2	3	4	5

From: S.A. Maisto, G.J. Connors, & R.L. Dearing: *Alcohol Use Disorders*   © 2007 Hogrefe & Huber Publishers

SITUATION	TEMPTED				
	Not at all	Not very	Moderately	Very	Extremely
16. When I sense everything is going wrong for me.	1	2	3	4	5
17. When people I used to drink with encourage me to drink.	1	2	3	4	5
18. When I am feeling angry inside.	1	2	3	4	5
19. When I experience an urge or impulse to take a drink that catches me unprepared.	1	2	3	4	5
20. When I am excited or celebrating with others.	1	2	3	4	5

We would like you to take another look at these 20 situations and think now about how *confident* you are in your ability to abstain from drinking in these situations. Please circle the number in each column that best describes your feelings of *confidence in your ability to abstain from drinking* in each situation *at the present time* according to the 1 to 5 scale provided.

SITUATION	CONFIDENT				
	Not at all	Not very	Moderately	Very	Extremely
1. When I am in agony because of stopping or withdrawing from alcohol use.	1	2	3	4	5
2. When I have a headache.	1	2	3	4	5
3. When I am feeling depressed.	1	2	3	4	5
4. When I am on vacation and want to relax.	1	2	3	4	5
5. When I am concerned about someone.	1	2	3	4	5
6. When I am very worried.	1	2	3	4	5
7. When I have the urge to try just one drink to see what happens.	1	2	3	4	5
8. When I am being offered a drink in a social situation.	1	2	3	4	5
9. When I dream about taking a drink.	1	2	3	4	5

From: S.A. Maisto, G.J. Connors, & R.L. Dearing: *Alcohol Use Disorders* © 2007 Hogrefe & Huber Publishers

SITUATION	CONFIDENT				
	Not at all	Not very	Moderately	Very	Extremely
10. When I want to test my willpower over drinking.	1	2	3	4	5
11. When I am feeling a physical need or craving for alcohol.	1	2	3	4	5
12. When I am physically tired.	1	2	3	4	5
13. When I am experiencing some physical pain or injury.	1	2	3	4	5
14. When I feel like blowing up because of frustration.	1	2	3	4	5
15. When I see others drinking at a bar or at a party.	1	2	3	4	5
16. When I sense everything is going wrong for me.	1	2	3	4	5
17. When people I used to drink with encourage me to drink.	1	2	3	4	5
18. When I am feeling angry inside.	1	2	3	4	5
19. When I experience an urge or impulse to take a drink that catches me unprepared.	1	2	3	4	5
20. When I am excited or celebrating with others.	1	2	3	4	5

Daily Drinking Diary

Use this form to keep track of when, where, and exactly how much you drink. Make a separate entry for each time that you drink. For example, if you have two drinks at a bar and then another drink after you get home, list these as two separate entries. In the column labeled Consequences, write down both good and bad consequences of your drinking. You can also use this column to jot down your thoughts and mood while drinking. Be sure to bring your Daily Drinking Diary to your sessions with your therapist.

Date and Time	Situation (e.g., where, who are you with, thoughts, moods, etc.)	Amount Consumed (type of beverages and number of standard drinks)	Consequences (e.g., positive or negative outcomes, thoughts, moods, etc.)

From: S.A. Maisto, G.J. Connors, & R.L. Dearing: *Alcohol Use Disorders*   © 2007 Hogrefe & Huber Publishers

Worksheet for Functional Analysis of Drinking Behavior

Antecedents (What was the context? Where were you? Who was there? Day and time? How were you feeling? What were you thinking?)	Drinking Behavior (What and how much did you consume? Over what period of time?)	Consequences (positive and/or negative outcomes, including your behavior, thoughts, moods, feelings, relationships with others, and so on)	
		Short-Term	Long-Term

From: S.A. Maisto, G.J. Connors, & R.L. Dearing: *Alcohol Use Disorders*   © 2007 Hogrefe & Huber Publishers

Alcohol Use Disorders Identification Test (AUDIT)

1. How often do you have a drink containing alcohol?

| Never | Monthly or less | Two to four times a month | Two to three times a week | Four or more times a week |

2. How many drinks containing alcohol do you have on a typical day when you are drinking?

| 1 or 2 | 3 or 4 | 5 or 6 | 7 to 9 | 10 or more |

3. How often do you have six or more drinks on one occasion?

| Never | Less than monthly | Monthly | Weekly | Daily or almost daily |

4. How often during the last year have you found that you were not able to stop drinking once you had started?

| Never | Less than monthly | Monthly | Weekly | Daily or almost daily |

5. How often during the last year have you failed to do what was normally expected from you because of drinking?

| Never | Less than monthly | Monthly | Weekly | Daily or almost daily |

6. How often during the last year have you needed a first drink in the morning to get yourself going after a heavy drinking session?

| Never | Less than monthly | Monthly | Weekly | Daily or almost daily |

7. How often during the last year have you had a feeling of guilt or remorse after drinking?

| Never | Less than monthly | Monthly | Weekly | Daily or almost daily |

8. How often during the last year have you been unable to remember what happened the night before because you had been drinking?

| Never | Less than monthly | Monthly | Weekly | Daily or almost daily |

9. Have you or someone else been injured as a result of your drinking?

| No | Yes, but not in the last year | Yes, during the last year |

10. Has a relative or friend, or a doctor or other health worker been concerned about your drinking or suggested you cut down?

| No | Yes, but not in the last year | Yes, during the last year |

From: S.A. Maisto, G.J. Connors, & R.L. Dearing: *Alcohol Use Disorders*   © 2007 Hogrefe & Huber Publishers

Past Month Alcohol Use Among Women

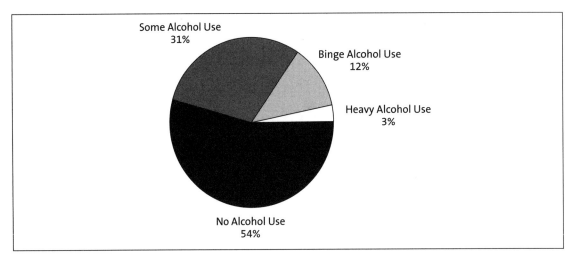

No Alcohol Use = Less than one drink on a single occasion in the past 30 days.
Some Alcohol Use = At least one drink on a single occasion in the past 30 days.
Binge Alcohol Use = Five or more drinks on the same occasion at least once in the past 30 days.
Heavy Alcohol Use = Five or more drinks on the same occasion on each of 5 (or more) days in the past 30 days. (All heavy alcohol users could also be categorized as binge alcohol users.)

Past Month Alcohol Use Among Men

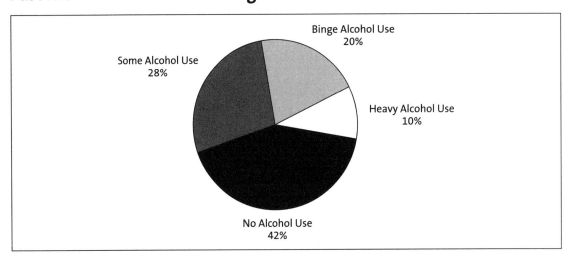

No Alcohol Use = Less than one drink on a single occasion in the past 30 days.
Some Alcohol Use = At least one drink on a single occasion in the past 30 days.
Binge Alcohol Use = Five or more drinks on the same occasion at least once in the past 30 days.
Heavy Alcohol Use = Five or more drinks on the same occasion on each of 5 (or more) days in the past 30 days. (All heavy alcohol users could also be categorized as binge alcohol users.)

Data based on 2005 National Survey on Drug Use and Health (Substance Abuse and Mental Health Services Administration, 2005).

High-Risk for Drinking Situations – Identification and Coping Strategies

On the left side of this form, list your potential high-risk for drinking situations. A high-risk situation is any event, thought, situation, place, person, etc., that is associated with my previous drinking and thus represents a risk for future drinking. Then, on the right side, list the coping strategies you will be able to use to deal with *each* of these high-risk situations.

High-Risk Situation   **Coping Strategies**

1. _____   _____
                                      _____
                                      _____

2. _____   _____
                                      _____
                                      _____

3. _____   _____
                                      _____
                                      _____

4. _____   _____
                                      _____
                                      _____

5. _____   _____
                                      _____
                                      _____

6. _____   _____
                                      _____
                                      _____

From: S.A. Maisto, G.J. Connors, & R.L. Dearing: *Alcohol Use Disorders*   © 2007 Hogrefe & Huber Publishers

What To Do if a Relapse Occurs

1. Use the relapse as a learning experience.

2. See the relapse as a specific, unique event.

3. Examine the relapse openly in order to reduce the amount of guilt and/or shame you may feel (those thoughts can lead to a feeling of hopelessness and continued drinking).

4. Analyze the triggers for the relapse.

5. Examine what the expectations about drinking were at the time (What did you anticipate drinking would accomplish in that situation?).

6. Plan for dealing with the aftermath/consequences of the relapse.

7. Tell yourself that control is only a moment away.

8. Renew your commitment to abstinence.

9. Make immediate plans for recovery – don't hesitate, do it now!

10. Contact your counselor and discuss slips in your aftercare session.

From: S.A. Maisto, G.J. Connors, & R.L. Dearing: *Alcohol Use Disorders*   © 2007 Hogrefe & Huber Publishers

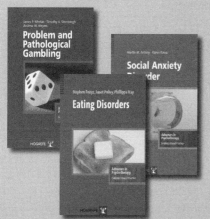

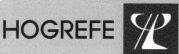

Advances in Psychotherapy – Evidence-Based Practice

Developed and edited in consultation with the Society of Clinical Psychology (APA Division 12).

Pricing / Standing Order Terms

Regular Prices: Single volume – US $ / € 24.95; Series Standing Order – US $ / € 19.95
APA D12 member prices: Single volume – $19.95; Series Standing Order – $17.95
With a Series Standing Order you will automatically be sent each new volume upon its release. After a minimum of 4 successive volumes, the Series Standing Order can be cancelled at any time. If you wish to pay by credit card, we will hold the details on file but your card will only be charged when a new volume actually ships.

Order Form (please check a box)

☐ I would like to place a Standing Order for the series at the special price of US $ / € 19.95 per volume, starting with volume no. ....

☐ I am a D12 Member and would like to place a Standing Order for the series at the special D12 Member Price of US $17.95 per volume, starting with volume no. ......
My APA membership no. is:

☐ I would like to order the following single volumes at the regular price of US $ / € 24.95 per volume.

☐ I am a D12 Member and would like to order the following single volumes at the special D12 Member Price of US $19.95 per volume.
My APA D12 membership no. is:

Qty.	Author / Title / ISBN	Price	Total
		Subtotal	
	WA residents add 8.8% sales tax		
	Shipping & handling:		
	USA — US $6.00 per volume (multiple copies: US $1.25 for each further copy)		
	Canada — US $8.00 per volume (multiple copies: US $2.00 for each further copy)		
	South America: — US $10.00 per volume (multiple copies: US $2.00 for each further copy)		
	Europe: — € 6.00 per volume (multiple copies: € 1.25 for each further copy)		
	Rest of the World: — € 8.00 per volume (multiple copies: € 1.50 for each further copy)		
		Total	

[ ] Check enclosed [ ] Please bill me Charge my: [ ] VISA [ ] MC [ ] AmEx

Card # _____ CVV2/CVC2/CID # _____ Exp date _____

Signature _____

Shipping address (please include phone & fax) _____

_____

_____

_____

_____

Order online at: **www.hhpub.com** or call toll-free **(800) 228-3749**
please quote "APT 2007" when ordering

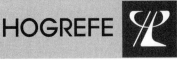

HOGREFE

Hogrefe & Huber Publishers · 30 Amberwood Parkway · Ashland, OH 44805
Tel: (800) 228-3749 · Fax: (419) 281-6883
Hogrefe & Huber Publishers · Rohnsweg 25 · D-37085 Göttingen
Tel: +49 551 49 609-0 · Fax: +49 551 49 609-88
E-Mail: custserv@hogrefe.com